PRAISE

THAT WHICH DOESN'T KILL US

"The Blooms' memoir addresses some of the most prevalent challenges that are present in nearly all committed relationships. *That Which Doesn't Kill Us* is destined to become a classic in the genre of relationship literature. It's a real page-turner and hard to put down. Charlie and Linda reveal through their ruthless honesty, the details of what caused them to sink so low and how they were able to salvage what appeared to be a "dead on arrival" marriage. This book is gripping, compelling, and inspiring. Ignore its teachings at your peril!"
~ Gerald Jampolsky, MD, and Diane Cirincione-Jampolsky, PhD,
co-authors of
Aging With Attitude

"Linda and Charlie Bloom's honest account of their heart-wrenching and redemptive journey moved me deeply. It left me with hope that when I come to places in my marriage that seem dead-ends, if I'm willing to keep opening up to what's possible—I just might find myself in a relationship so beautiful—it was simply unimaginable. This book will stay with you for years to come. A gem—thank you!"
~ Renee Trudeau, author of
*The Mother's Guide to Self-Renewal:
How to Reclaim, Rejuvenate and Re-Balance Your Life*

"A high-five to the Blooms for their searchingly—sometimes searingly—honest portrayal of love and togetherness, for telling it like it is and not pulling any punches. Their blazing honesty and articulateness about their process of coming apart and coming together not only makes for page-turner, but it is ultimately a tribute to the hard human work of making love last.

Their book is an eye-opener and a ripping good read."
~ Gregg Levoy, author of
Vital Signs

"This book takes the reader on a journey of pathos and passion, conflict and commitment, love and hate, and shows us the inseparability of things usually thought to be in contradiction to one another. Don't miss this one if you want a deep experience of how long-lasting love really feels!"
~ Susan Campbell, PhD, author of
Five Minute Relationship Repair

"*That Which Doesn't Kill Us* reads like a gripping novel. It is both raw and profoundly intimate, dealing with relational issues that most readers will easily identify with. It is a story of redemption; of how a couple can descend into the darkest pits of hell and manage to find their way out with an even deeper ever-growing commitment to their relationship. I highly recommend this book to everyone. And it gives us hope for great happiness and peace if we take this ride all the way to its end."
~ Alanna Brogan, MSN, PHN, RN, Professor
Faculty at Sonoma State University

"This book is an extraordinary accomplishment . . . not just to examine such painful memories in order to share them publicly so that others may benefit, but to do so with such searing honesty and humbleness and raw emotion that there is no doubt of the authenticity of their shared journey. Charlie and Linda are both remarkable therapists, authors and workshop leaders because of their past suffering and redemption. This book is not for the fainthearted, but then relationship never is."
~ Denise Barak, Director of Program Innovation
Kripalu Center

"With vulnerability, transparency and courage, Linda and Charlie Bloom invite us to watch the movie of their marriage, day by day, from reel to real. A touching and authentic collaboration, this book will inspire you to go the distance with your own relationship—until you receive the full abundance of its emotional and spiritual gifts!"

~ Daphne Rose Kingma, author of
The Future of Love

"There's so much to say about this remarkable book. Once, I began. I couldn't stop reading. Each page brought me closer to myself, my own history, my partner, and most importantly to an understanding of the times that have shaped our ability to connect intimately with one another. We each and all need this book right now!"

~ Dawna Markova PhD, author of
Reconcilable Differences: Connecting in a Disconnected World

"*That Which Doesn't Kill Us* provides an intimate and vulnerable view of a relationship between husband and wife which becomes entangled, lost and at a place of personal and relational survival, that is finally reborn. As I read the Bloom's story of their relationship and personal struggles, I found myself opening up my own heart and falling back deeply in love with my wife. This book gave me a better understanding of my own barricades to receiving and expressing love. Charlie and Linda's openness gave me the courage to look more deeply at my own life. This book is a must-read for anyone who wants to transform their life and relationships."

~ Gary Fagin, MD

"It is rare that we get a deep glimpse into the authentic inner and interpersonal world of a couple. Through their courageous vulnerability, the Blooms take on the inner sanctum of the relationship—showing us how working with our fears, hopes, hurts, and traumas can lead to personal and spiritual transformation. The Blooms show us how remaining committed to the marital process can reward us with a deep and rich connection born of soulful struggle."

~ John Amodeo, PhD, author of
Dancing with Fire

"Finally, a book by a couple who not only captivates us by a good story but also teaches us much about real love. And you get an extra bonus, hearing the story and learned relationship lessons from the perspective of both partners."

~ Barry Vissell, MD, and Joyce Vissell, RN, MS, co-authors of
The Shared Heart and *Light in the Mirror*

"I found Charlie and Linda's story moving and courageous of both of them to be willing to put themselves out there in the way that they have way. People who are struggling in relationship will gain a lot from their story, and learn that it is what we endure that inspires our relationship to be what it can be."

~ Maya Spector, author of
The Persephone Cycle

"Linda and Charlie Bloom are master teachers and highly gifted writers. In their astonishing new book, *That Which Doesn't Kill Us,* you will meet them–warts and all. This auto-vivisection of their subconscious minds is a gift to humanity. Traversing the colorful landscape of their relationship from the male and female perspective is both harrowing and enlightening."

~ Ira Israel, author of
How to Survive Your Childhood Now That You're an Adult

"The Blooms have written a book about devastation, recovery, and transcendence. In this tale, the dual devastations of addiction, depression, and cancer are the broken places and crucibles for personal and marital transformation."

~ David Kerns, MD, author of
Standard of Care

"In *That Which Doesn't Kill Us* Linda and Charlie Bloom courageously share details of turbulent times when the survival of their own marriage was at stake. Their story is poignant, fascinating, and inspiring!"

~ Marcia Naomi Berger, author of
Marriage Meetings for Lasting Love

"*That Which Doesn't Kill Us* contains the seeds of wisdom, truth and inspiration. It is a must-read for couples of any age."

~ Ken Druck, PhD, author of
Courageous Aging: Your Best Years Ever Reimagined

THAT WHICH DOESN'T KILL US

How One Couple Became Stronger at the Broken Places

To Patricia and James:
May you constantly be
surrounded by love:
Many Blessings:
Linda Bloom

CHARLIE AND LINDA BLOOM

ISBN: 978-0-9965785-5-4
ISBN: 0-9965785-5-2
Library of Congress Control Number: 2017959050

Cover and text design: Miko Radcliffe

Sacred Life Publishers™
SacredLife.com
Printed in the United States of America

CONTENTS

FOREWORD

"Why do relationships have to be so hard?" It's a question that many therapists, particularly marriage counselors, hear a lot. Of course, not every relationship demands extra attention and hard work—at least not all the time! Still, many or most couple relationships will go through times of stress and even crisis; and often in these times we're surprised—maybe bewildered and alarmed as well—by how fast a seemingly small difference can spiral down and out, sometimes calling into question our very future itself as partners.

There are good reasons why many of us choose partners with very different personality styles from our own, different traditions or expectations, or even different values. Often the irony is that we've chosen each other partly for those very differences: "She's so organized, so responsible!" or "He's so spontaneous, so open to new things!" These new capacities may seem and be so desirable, with each partner bringing something the other very much needs—and needs to learn. Then later on, under new life commitments and new stresses and challenges, I may come to feel that these same features that were so attractive to me then have somehow morphed now into issues that divide us, even threaten to tear the marriage apart. How do we live through these times—and not just get through them, not just paper over the conflict and avoid it going forward, but really hang in there and really reach deeper into ourselves and toward each other amid pain and fears? And then how do we come out larger, stronger, with new understanding and new capacities, not just surviving but thriving, laying the groundwork for a new life phase of change, intimacy, and growth?

This book tells the story of one couple in early midlife—Linda and Charlie Bloom—who were attracted to each other both for their shared passions and dreams and for those very different styles, different energies each of them brought to the relationship, and each saw in the other. In the alternating voices of each partner, they take us with them on an intimate journey through their marriage, including one critical, at times agonizing, year, moving deep into an abyss of stress and challenge that went right to the edge of breaking up their family and then back again to stronger, richer lives both as individuals and as a couple.

But wait, you may say at this point. Doesn't our individualistic culture teach us at every turn that these things—personal dreams and fulfillment, on one hand, and deep, intimate relationship, on the other—are polar opposites, locked in a kind of zero-sum game in which the more I get of one, the less I have (or my partner has) of the other! That there's a finite amount of love, support, and freedom available, and those fixed quantities inevitably get sliced up between us so that when push comes to shove (and push will definitely come to shove), we end up fighting over that last slice of something precious and seemingly rare. And then won't we just either go on bickering (or worse) endlessly, or at any rate until one or the other just gives up?

Well, yes, those myths are out there: our culture often does seem to be telling us, indirectly and sometimes directly, that in the end a relationship is a kind of push-me, pull-you, an unnatural creature that may bring you certain things you desire and need (sex, security, children, relief of loneliness) but at the terrible price of your freedom and of fulfilling your personal dreams.

But don't you believe those myths—because that's all they are: myths! You have only to read the chapters ahead of you now in this amazing book to experience something deeper, newer, more revelatory. Tender highs and excruciating lows, yes, and all through it a wrenching, vulnerable honesty, a kind of raw nakedness that reflects a larger strength and confidence in the sharing. We recognize ourselves in these chapters: not that we've necessarily gone to those same extremes of words and feelings (or maybe we have), but most of us have felt those feelings and have reached those limits of hopelessness or panic. Perhaps most often the relationship where we felt those things didn't make it, and we may still carry the scars, even some unhealed places from those searing experiences that the daring experiment of intimacy and vulnerability may bring.

And isn't that the larger danger: that where those old hurts and fears have not so much healed as scarred over. We may have learned a kind of avoidance of certain places, certain vulnerable exposures, because of old fear and pain. And in the process, we may be stepping around or holding ourselves back from the kind of intimacy we once dreamed of—and as a result missing opportunities for growth both as individuals and as a couple.

Because the real truth of this book—and of our oh-so-human lives—is that the self and relationships are not opposite poles of our being at all. Rather, these two kinds of experience stand in a kind of dynamic "figure–ground" relationship with each other: each one potentially providing the grounding for new growth, a new flourishing in the other "pole" of our being. Finding the courage to reach deeper once more in my most vulnerable, most intimately exposed relationship can serve as the springboard for a new opening in personal growth, in other family and friendship relations, and in my life at work and in the world. And in the same way, a stronger, more open creativity in those other dimensions of my life can serve to enhance, not compete with, my primary couple relationship.

But where do I find the courage for these new risks, new "moves" that likely carry vulnerability and at least a certain sense of risk? Well, I'd say one terrific place to start is with this book. Charlie and Linda Bloom have been there, to the darkest places of relational despair, and they've come back stronger, more creative, more courageous for the journey, which now they offer to us.

For many years the Blooms have shared their skills and wisdom and experience with many hundreds of clients and workshop participants—and then through their books and blogs, with thousands more. In the process they've given us many lessons and told us many stories of other couples. Now they give us a deep dive into their own.

What will you learn from this profound sharing? Well, that will be for you to say. For me, among so many other things I learned—again—the huge truths that vulnerability is strength, that humility is power, and that my greatest fears, my greatest desires, my deepest wounds, and, yes, my greatest creativity and gifts all lie in the same places. And this: that the deepest courage comes not from inside myself alone: it comes from spirited companionship. This book gives us that intimate, accepting companionship, two fellow travelers for my journey. And while they can't take my journey for me, I can take theirs with them in this retelling, and in the end that will be the clearest, most impactful teaching for my own.

Thank you, Linda and Charlie Bloom, for the gift of this precious, painful, ultimately inspiring, and, finally, quietly triumphant tale, this creation of more love in the universe out of your own pain and your own love. I'm encouraged for my own journey (in the literal sense, of encouraged)—as a partner, as a parent and friend, as a professional, and as a man—by the gift. I believe you will be too.

Gordon Wheeler
Esalen Institute, Big Sur California

Chapter 1

BECOMING A BELIEVER

Charlie

Our deterioration from a reasonably functional middle-class family to a disintegrating cluster of struggling survivors took about six months. It began in February 1982 in Connecticut, where Linda and I, and our children, Jesse (7), Eben (3), and Sarah (1) had been living for the previous seven years. Linda and I had recently celebrated our ninth wedding anniversary. Connecticut had just emerged from one of the most brutal winters in New England history. There had been weeks of unrelenting, record-breaking freezing weather and massive amounts of snow and ice. Four days after my thirty-fifth birthday, I found myself lying in bed, having thrown out my back shoveling my car out of a huge blizzard that had paralyzed traffic in most of the Northeast.

With every movement of my arms or legs, I experienced excruciatingly painful spasms which threw me into a kind of voluntary paralysis, so I tried to eliminate any unnecessary movement that might send me into excruciating spasms of agony. Consumed by self-pity, frustration, and anger, I found one word continually replaying itself in my mind: "Enough."

Although as a kid I had loved winter, as an adult, for me, the months between October and May had become wearisome. Three years before, after returning from a two-week trip to San Francisco, I had promised Linda that it would be only a very short time before we moved to the West Coast. The idea of living in a place where walking around outdoors in midwinter wearing nothing more than a T-shirt, jeans, and running shoes was immensely enticing to us. As I lay in bed nursing my back in a house that our wood stove couldn't adequately heat, it became clear to me that the time had come to get out of New England and, at last, fulfill the dream that had possessed us since our first visit to the West Coast in 1969. Until then, the idea of moving to California had seemed more like a fantasy than a real possibility. We were entrenched in our little rural town, and to think of leaving the comfort and security of our life there for the uncertainty, competitiveness, and expense of California was daunting.

The shift from fantasy to possibility had actually begun the previous September. At the urging of a friend, I had enrolled in a personal growth seminar in New York City. During the five-day workshop, I had uncovered a deep desire for a change in my life that I had been denying out of fear of jeopardizing the structured life that Linda and I had carefully created together. The change that I was looking for required more than a change in scenery or weather. It was about something much bigger.

Since accepting a position at a mental health clinic shortly after completing graduate school in Boston in 1975 I had been working as a therapist and a private practitioner, and I was beginning to feel burned out. Although I was a decent therapist, my heart was no longer in the work the way it used to be, but I was unwilling to admit that to myself or to anyone else, for that matter. The consequences of doing so would have been too disruptive to the life that Linda and I had strived so hard to create. Unbeknownst to me, all that was about to change.

My friend Richard, a psychiatrist who worked at the clinic with me, was the one who stirred the hornet's nest after he did a personal growth training that, in his words, "completely turned my life around." Like me, Richard had been struggling with ambivalent feelings about his career and had just completed an intensive five-day seminar; he had returned home convinced that he had finally found the elixir for which he had been seeking. He also came back convinced that I needed to do the training and that I would find the answer to my question about the next step in my career and life, just as he had.

"This is it," he told me. "This is what we've been looking for. I knew that something out there would unlock the door to my heart, and this is it. I'm absolutely clear that I'm going to go to work for this company as a trainer, and after you do the training, you'll want to, as well. You'll see. I guarantee it!"

Having a tendency toward skepticism as I do, Richard's extreme enthusiasm not only didn't persuade me to join him in his enthusiasm; it had the opposite effect. It put me off and activated my mistrust of people and groups who seemed lost in euphoria and wild-eyed exuberance. I felt coerced by what seemed to be a lot of hype that Richard had been fed and swallowed. Listening to his superlatives about his experience set off alarms in my head. Though I wouldn't go so far as to say he had been brainwashed, I seriously doubted that Richard had seen the truth and the light. I decided to wait and see whether he actually followed up on all his new, enthusiastic intentions.

To my surprise, he did. Richard not only fulfilled his predictions; he also surpassed them. Over the next several months, he resigned his position at the clinic, got hired by the company, moved to California, completed the trainers' training program, reunited with and remarried his ex-wife, and brought her and their two children to the West Coast to live with him. In less than a year, he was promoted to the position of director of training and became solidly entrenched in the hierarchy of the company.

During this time, Richard and I remained in close communication. With a combination of envy and awe I watched him transform his life. By the summer of 1981 I had seen enough, yet despite the changes that I observed him making in his personal and professional life, I remained skeptical, waiting for the other shoe to drop. It never did. Finally, I realized that I had seen enough to believe the validity of what Richard had been telling me. There was no question that he and his life had substantially and radically changed. He also seemed to have changed as a person. In July I called the company's New York center and reserved a place for myself in the next seminar.

On the day of the training I took a train to New York and a cab to the hotel where it was being held. Richard had warned me not to be late, a long-term behavioral problem of mine he had noticed. "It would be a bad way to get started," he told me. I arrived at the hotel nearly an hour before registration began, and several people were already manning the registration tables. They were mostly young, in their twenties and thirties, well dressed; and were all smiling, wide-eyed, and excited. Their enthusiasm only activated my skeptical thoughts that were returning now that I was on the verge of actually doing the training. I found a chair away from the registration table but strategically located so that I could observe the arrival of the other students.

At precisely 8 p.m., the doors to the room opened with an announcement from a staff person: "Doors are open; come in and take a seat." It sounded more like a command than a request. Once in the room, we were told to fill the seats, starting with the front row and working our way to the back. So much for hiding out.

Richard had warned me that I might have an impulse to leave in the early stages of the training, and he got me to agree to hang in until the end. Had I not given him my word, I'm almost certain that I would have left before the night was over. After we were seated, two of the people sitting at the staff table at the back of the room closed the doors. I noticed that serious expressions seeming to convey that playtime was over had replaced their smiles. It was time to get down to business.

The room suddenly went totally silent, even though no one told us not to talk. A few moments later a man stepped up to the front of the room, introduced himself as Jay, and informed us that he would be our trainer. Jay appeared to be in his mid-thirties. He was immaculately dressed and strikingly handsome. He welcomed us to the seminar and told us that, before the training could actually begin, there was the matter of ground rules to which we all would have to agree.

"This can go quick and easy, or you can make it difficult," he told us. "The ground rules are the rules of the game. They speak for themselves. They don't change. No exceptions. There is no negotiating them. No discussion. You must agree to every one of them in order to be in the training. If you choose not to agree to any of them, you will need to leave. You cannot get your money back. Any questions? Good. Let's begin."

Despite Jay's insistence that there would be no exceptions made for anyone under any conditions to alter the ground rules, there was an ongoing series of attempts made by students to cajole, coerce, and otherwise attempt to get him to grant exceptions to the rules—all without success. After nearly three hours of "processing," the ground rules were finally accepted by the group, minus three of the nearly 100 participants who had chosen to leave the training.

By the time Jay was finished with the rules, we had all signed away our rights to question the trainer's judgment, fold our arms, cross our legs, leave the room to go to the bathroom, or speak without permission. I felt insulted, controlled, degraded, and infantilized. During the break, I commiserated with several other students who had, like me, promised friends that they would give the training a chance. They, too, had been warned that they would probably feel a very strong urge to leave and promised that they would resist the temptation to go. Like me, their friends had assured them that by the end of the training they would be glad that they had stayed. The condition that the money-back guarantee was only good if you stayed for the entire training also did a lot to keep some of us from leaving that night.

I made up my mind to stay for the entire training, not just because I wanted to keep the option open to get a refund but because I was deeply impressed with Jay's skill as a leader. Having done some group facilitation myself, I believed that I had a lot to learn from observing him in action. I also had a less conscious motivation for my decision to stay. I was beginning to feel that there really might be something important here for me, something that Richard had been trying to tell me that I hadn't been entirely open to receiving. I began thinking that there might be some value for me in at least temporarily suspending my judgments and skepticism. The thought was both intriguing and unsettling. While I was disturbed by the authoritarian style of leadership that Jay had, I was impressed and moved by his sensitivity, humor, and obvious caring for the students. I felt a strong desire to experience the attention that he gave to each person with whom he spoke. Whether he was challenging someone or being challenged by someone, his demeanor was consistently steady, unwavering, and always compassionate. I felt envious of those students who challenged Jay, but I was unwilling to risk taking him on myself.

That night as I lay in bed reflecting on my experience, I thought about dropping the skepticism that I so often felt whenever I considered accepting a point of view that was incongruent with my usual perspective. I thought about Jay's invitation to be open to the possibility that this experience could literally be life-changing. Wasn't that what I was looking for? All I would have to do to find out if that really was true was to choose to drop my defenses for the next four days and trust the training, the trainer, and, most importantly, myself. That night I decided, in the jargon of the training, to "go for it."

The next day, having surrendered much—but not all—of my "resistance" my experience shifted from feeling tense, anxious, and apprehensive to being more relaxed, lighter, and enthusiastic. I also noticed that I was becoming increasingly more impressed with Jay's level of skill and care. His insightfulness and eloquence were truly extraordinary. I kept thinking to myself, "I can't believe how good this guy is!"

The structure of the training included short lectures on subjects that were relevant to most peoples' lives, including, relationships, self-trust and interpersonal trust, risk taking, self-esteem, intentionality, accountability, and responsibility. After every lecture, Jay would put us in an experiential exercise that allowed us to personalize the distinctions that he made regarding each topic. These exercises were done with a partner, in a small group, the whole group, or individually, usually with eyes closed. During the exercises and throughout most of the training, music was played that served to intensify any emotions that arose during the process. A third part of the training was "sharing," which refers to a debriefing of feelings and insights that were provoked through the exercises. Sharing could take place with a partner, in a small group, or while standing in the front of the whole group speaking into a microphone.

With each passing day of the training I became more impressed with the transformative changes that I was observing in the other students and in myself, as well. I felt increasingly more comfortable in my own skin: more accepting and openhearted toward others, less aloof, less judgmental, and more connected to others. I hadn't even realized how much I needed this shift in my way of being. I laughed and cried more during those five days than I had in years, and it all felt good, even the tears.

As the training drew to a close, I knew that I wanted more. I was convinced that this experience was far more powerful than any form of life enrichment I had ever seen. Jay reminded us that this wasn't the end of the journey; it was just the beginning. He talked about the advanced training that he promised would take us much further than this one did and would open us to literally inconceivable possibilities. Whatever that cost, I was in.

The closing ceremony was held on Sunday evening. We formed a circle and closed our eyes while friends and family members were quietly ushered into the room and soft music played in the background. I could hear the guests coming into the room and their whisperings. I didn't expect to see anyone I knew, but when Jay instructed us to open our eyes, to my surprise, I saw not only Richard but also Linda, our three children, and my best friend, Allan, who happened to be visiting from the West Coast. I was so overwhelmed with emotion that my knees went weak and I almost collapsed. I kept repeating the words "Thank you" to Richard, over and over.

In five days, I had done a complete turnaround. My previous concerns and criticisms had dissolved into an experience of oceanic bliss more potent than any infatuation I'd ever experienced. I was in love—deeply, completely, and ecstatically in love with life, with the people in my life, and with myself. The training had made good on all of its promises, implicit and explicit, to give me a life that was truly and fully worth living. Not a hollow, shallow version that I had thought was "it," but this—this was it, and I got it!

After some tearful goodbyes, Linda, the kids, and I packed ourselves into the car for the two-and-a-half-hour drive home. The kids immediately fell asleep, but I couldn't stop talking while Linda drove. During the drive I poured out some of the denied and unexpressed feelings that the training had awakened in me. I told Linda that I was grateful beyond words to have her in my life. She had hung in there with me despite what I now saw was the arrogance and self-righteousness that I had used to shield myself from my deeper feelings. I pledged to never again hurt or disrespect her in the ways that I saw I had. "I'd rather cut off my own arm than cause you any pain," I said. "I know that you know that I've been taking you for granted, but I swear to you, those days are over. That will never happen again. You're the best thing that's ever happened to me, and I'll never forget it."

Even as I spoke those words, a voice in the back of my mind asked who I thought I was kidding. "Sure, you mean this now, but when the smoke clears, it'll be back to business as usual. You'll forget again, just like you always do." Although I'd never experienced anything like this, I'd made and broken enough promises for Linda to know that there was a better than even chance that my enthusiasm would eventually wear off. There had been too many times over the years that I had, upon acknowledging my verbal abuse or neglect of Linda, promised to change and then returned within days to my old patterns. Why Linda had put up with these endless cycles was a mystery to me. My track record was abysmal.

But all that was about to change. In fact, my whole life was soon going to be totally different. "That sounds great," Linda finally said after I paused long enough to come up for air. "But I've heard this before, and despite your sincerity, it's hard for me to trust that things are really going to change."

"I'm going to work for the company. I'm going to be a trainer. We're finally going to fulfill our dream of living in California. I feel like I've been waiting my whole life for this, and I've finally found it. I know that if I'm spending my time around people like Jay, there's no way that I'm going to keep slipping back into my old shit anymore. That's the missing link to the puzzle: support. I've never had the kind of support that's required to break these old habits and patterns, but if I'm hanging out with people like him, there'll be no way that I'll keep falling back into my old stuff."

An hour out of the training and one more time I was again already trying to coerce Linda into buying my latest scheme. This time it was about us giving up practically everything in our lives and moving to California. When I sensed that she didn't seem to be buying it, I redoubled my efforts, thinking that if I raised the heat, she would see things my way, the *right* way.

"I realize it's impossible for you to appreciate the power of the training, but you'll see. You'll recognize it in the changes that you're going to see in me. I have learned something that I'm certain is going to have a permanent impact on my life. You'll see for yourself when you do the training. This organization is doing the work that we've wanted to do for years, and they're doing it at a state-of-the-art level. All that I ask is that you give me a chance to prove that every word I'm saying is true. I promise, you won't regret it."

Linda did give me a chance. By the end of the year we had both completed the Basic Course, the Advanced Course, and the Leadership Program. We'd invested over $4,000 in tuition, not counting what we'd spent on transportation to New York a few times a month, astronomical phone bills, and additional childcare costs.

But money was no object. Linda caught the fever, and the two of us spun out in a frenzied adrenaline rush, continually pumping each other and ourselves up with near-manic enthusiasm. Our friends and family were also subject to our impassioned pleas to do the training, and several of them were so turned off that they refused to have anything to do with us unless we agreed to stop pestering them. Most of the other people in our leadership programs—we were in separate groups—were having similar problems, and much of our dialogue centered on ways we could more effectively deal with the "resistance" we were encountering from our uninitiated friends.

In some cases, the consequence of our persistence was long periods of alienation and resentment. A few of our friendships never fully recovered "Sometimes," we were told by our group leaders, "you have to be willing to risk your relationship with someone if you really care about them." The guise of supporting our friends and family members to "handle their considerations" meant "Don't let them buy into their own excuses and get them to enroll." We were encouraged to risk being overbearing if necessary to get people to do the training, to "make a difference in their lives and in the world."

In January, after Linda and I had completed our programs, we both crashed. The stimulation and distraction of the game had worn off, leaving me with a depressingly flat, monotonously predictable reality with no exciting challenges to motivate me. Although I missed the adrenaline rush of the game, my body was exhausted from sleep deprivation and overwork, and I had a lot of catching up to do. I had been neglecting my practice and just sliding by doing the bare minimum at the local state college where I was doing some part-time teaching. The kids were tired of being hustled from one babysitter to another. It was time to pull in and slow down.

I had seen some of the shadow side of the company, and it wasn't pretty. While the party line was about "making a difference in the world," the unspoken message was always about "enrollments," which translated as money. It smelled bad.

In February I got a call from Richard. He wanted to know if I was interested in becoming a trainer. When I expressed reluctance, he shifted into hyper sales mode. His argument was that it was a whole new ball game. "I've just been promoted to director of trainings for the company. That means that I have complete authority to implement what you and I both know this company needs in order to clean everything up and set things straight. We're going to put the crisis behind us and see to it that it stays there forever."

The "crisis" that Richard was referring to was a piece of investigative reporting that had recently been aired on national TV about the trainings. It portrayed the company as a dangerous cult that was out to convert as many people as possible to a perverse form of New Age spirituality. The show stated that a number of people had died as a result of reckless and irresponsible group leadership and that countless others experienced extreme psychological damage from the organization's often-successful brainwashing efforts. There was some degree of truth in the accusations, but most of them were grossly distorted. They were taken out of context and edited in a way that seemed to be intentionally designed to create an extremely negative impression of the company.

The fallout from the show was devastating to the company. Enrollments dropped drastically, several city offices closed, dozens of staff members were let go, and confused and angry graduates from all over the country were demanding an explanation. Multiple lawsuits threatened to overwhelm the organization's legal staff, and the company was in danger of collapsing. In an effort to stem the bloodletting, the company instituted changes in the training designed to make itself less vulnerable to public attack.

Promoting Richard, a board-certified psychiatrist, to lead the training department had been a crucial step in that process. Putting him in charge of the trainings was another. Richard's unspoken job responsibility was to give the organization the professional credibility that it had never enjoyed. In addition, he was given the job of transforming the training by eliminating anything in it that could be interpreted as psychotherapy and putting an educational spin on it. Trainers would no longer be permitted to manipulate students into compliance by using intimidating and coercive tactics. Everything was to be "more professional, more mainstream."

The trainer body now needed to be reoriented to the new program. Richard's job was to either set the existing staff members straight or replace them if they weren't able to be set straight. None of the trainers had received the kind of training that Richard was talking about. Few had an academic or professional background in human relations. Those who couldn't make the grade would have to go. A new breed of facilitator, grounded in interpersonal and group dynamics, people who were more "trainable," would replace them.

Richard ended his pitch, saying, "I want you to come out and be a part of the new team. The old days are over. If the old guard can't handle these changes, they'll have to go. This transformation is a done deal. They'll either get on the bus or get out. I need you. The company needs you. I know that you've got reservations, but believe me we can make this work for you and for your family, too."

Even if I wanted the job, Richard didn't actually have the authority to hire me, only to recommend me. The company president and the trainer body would make the final decision after they interviewed me. I told him that I needed time to think about it and to talk to Linda. He told me the company was setting up a series of interviews the following month for about a dozen trainer candidates who were being flown in from around the country. He would need to know soon if I planned to be one of them. We agreed to talk again in a week.

The next day I decided to go for the job. Linda was 100 percent behind my decision. From a pragmatic standpoint, it seemed like a reckless, even irresponsible, move, but something about the excitement of stepping into what I suspected would be one of the hottest fires I'd ever encountered was compelling. The power of that challenge was a strong motivator in moving me toward the company. I felt a restless urgency to shake up my settled, secure life. A part of me was saying, "Take this step now! Make the move! If you don't, you'll forever regret it." Linda went out of her way to be as neutral as she could, reminding me that it was ultimately my decision and that she would support whatever I felt was right, but she admitted that she had a strong preference that I at least apply for the job.

Three weeks later I flew to San Francisco to participate in two days of interviews and other events orchestrated so that the other trainer candidates and I could be observed in more "informal" settings. As my flight arrived in San Francisco I was sick to my stomach and had a throbbing headache when I got off the plane. A volunteer was waiting for me at the baggage claim. He talked nonstop on our drive to the company's headquarters. When we arrived he showed me into a large room where several trainer candidates were awaiting their turn to be challenged, grilled, and interrogated by the review board, which consisted of the trainer body and the company president. The other candidates looked like slightly aging college athletes. They were tall and handsome, with an "all-American" look. I found them to be engaging, articulate, funny, and seemingly unselfconscious, everything I didn't seem to be.

When my turn came, I had a fleeting impulse to bolt out of the building and take a cab to the airport. "Better just to get out of here," I thought. "There's no way that I'm going to get this job. Why put myself through the humiliation of being rejected?" But I didn't even have the courage to do that, so I obediently went into the room and offered my head to the chopping block.

Oddly, it didn't go as badly as I had expected, perhaps, in part, because I had already taken the pressure off myself by letting go of my hope that I might be hired. The volunteer who had picked me up at the airport drove me to my hotel, and I flopped onto the bed, feeling very much alone and deflated

That night the company provided an elegant dinner for the trainers and the trainer candidates. My headache and upset stomach had finally dissipated, and I even felt somewhat relaxed. I flew home the next day and spent most of the flight identifying all the reasons that I really didn't want the job and listing all the good things about living out the rest of my days in rural Connecticut.

Three days after I returned from California, I got a phone call from Richard. He told me that he had been authorized to offer me the job. Hearing Richard's offer, I realized that my fear of disappointment had prevented me from admitting to myself just how badly I really did want it. "They want you to start in six weeks," Richard said.

I felt a sense of elation, followed almost immediately by a feeling of panic. Linda and I would have to sell our house and cars, terminate our practices, resign from our jobs, find a house in California, say goodbye to our friends and families, and start a new life three thousand miles away, all in less than two months. It seemed overwhelming, but I knew that somehow, we would be able to do it because I had done the training and because I knew that I was committed and that that would be enough. I also knew that my feelings wouldn't last forever and that I would eventually be able to relax again. I just had no idea how long it would be before I would.

Chapter 2

TRANSFORMATION

Charlie

Six weeks to the day after receiving the job offer, Linda, our three kids, and I landed at San Francisco International Airport with nothing but the luggage we carried onto the plane and moved into a rental house in a small town north of San Francisco. Five days later, the moving truck showed up carrying all our furniture and worldly possessions that we had not sold before the move. Two days after that, I was off to my first day of work, leaving Linda to unpack and bring order to our new home. This was the first of hundreds of times I left her to handle things while I heeded the call of the job.

I was soon informed, however, that what I had was not a "job" but a calling. The trainers all shared a belief that we had been accorded a magnificent honor: the opportunity to make an extraordinary contribution to the world. Consumed by such a burning mission, all other concerns pale in comparison: family, friends, recreation, even personal well-being. Everything is seen only in terms of the degree to which it serves the noble purpose of global transformation. Anyone fortunate enough to be offered this privilege becomes a part of an elite group, the Green Berets of consciousness.

I left my first staff meeting, and many others over the next five years, filled with inspiration and the fervor of a missionary, dedicated to bringing love and empowerment into the lives of others and into the world. I was thrilled to be a part of such a dramatic and far-reaching mission and was excited by the influence wielded by trainers. I knew that, more than anything, what I wanted was to feel what I knew the man in the front of the room was experiencing. He exuded complete confidence, certainty, strength, courage, and brilliance. What I saw was a master in the use of power, knowledge, and compassion.

The day after that first staff meeting, I said good-bye to Linda and the kids and got on a plane, along with the lead trainer, to Orange County, where I would participate in my first training as a newly minted trainer in training. Aside from feeling tormented with anxiety, getting very little sleep, and going half-crazy with relentless self-doubt, I managed to survive my first week in the training room. I was on the phone with Linda every night after we finished the evening session, typically after midnight. I poured out my feelings, trying to convey them to her, as if by doing so I could close the gap that already seemed to be opening between us.

One of the things I had found most compelling about the training was the way in which it seemed to bring a heightened intensity to life. To be in that room was to experience a rawness that wasn't present in my day-to-day life. I was somewhat of an adrenaline junkie and a sucker for that intensity. I loved the way the training made me feel so alive. What I didn't realize at the time was the effect this growing addiction would have on my life outside of work.

Theoretically, my work schedule called for me to be in the training room an average of two weeks a month—not a bad schedule even if one is working fourteen-hour days during the workweek. In practice, however, I put in considerably more time than that. For one thing, I actually averaged closer to three trainings a month in cities all over the country. Along with the five days in the training room, there were two travel days for most courses, two days of meetings, guest events, public presentations, and six or eight hours a month spent on reports, expense sheets, and assorted paperwork.

The little time I had available for activities outside of work was further compromised by my need to recover from my exhausting work schedule. Most weeks I flew home on the morning after the training and stopped in the office for the Monday meeting, which usually went most of the afternoon and often into the evening. When I finally got home, frequently after having eaten dinner, I was completely exhausted. It was often all I could do to stay awake during the thirty-minute drive from the office. Linda and the kids, if they were still awake, came out to greet me. As much as I enjoyed being reunited with them, I was so physically and emotionally spent that I was often too tired to be fully present. At first, their exuberance was a joy I delighted in. Over time, however, my limited ability and energy to respond took its toll.

After a week of marathon training on my part and single parenting on Linda's part, we each looked to the other for relief and support. In addition to wanting a break from her domestic responsibilities, Linda was also in need of the emotional connection we had shared before the move. Unlike me, practically all her time was spent with the kids. It would be a while before she developed the kind of adult friendships that sustained her. In the meantime, I was her sole source of adult connection, support, and caregiving. I knew how much more she needed me now, and I understood her situation, but what mattered most to me was the training.

During much of my nine months of training I felt overwhelmed by the challenge of mastering the training craft, and the last thing I wanted to do was worry about another needy person. I gave Linda and the kids what I could, but it was never enough. My life narrowed to a single focus: work. The other interests and activities that had been so much a part of my life in Connecticut were gone. I was, unknowingly, in the throes of an obsession that was consuming me.

My resistance to hearing Linda's complaints aggravated the situation. I didn't want to know about her needs, loneliness, anger, or exhaustion. It just made me feel guilty and inadequate. My tolerance for her feelings during my training period was low, not only because of my work schedule but also because I was focused on my own emotional survival. I had presumed that I would attain trainer status in four or five months, at the most, and would do it without much difficulty because I had a strong background in psychology and group dynamics. It soon became apparent that my professional background not only was unappreciated by the training staff but also was seen as a strong liability that I would have to overcome. The predominant message I received in staff meetings and from the senior facilitators was to "quit being a therapist. This isn't therapy."

I was constantly reminded that if I couldn't get with the program, I wouldn't make it. This was more than an idle threat. Trainer interns were routinely dismissed if they didn't make the grade. I had no idea what I would do if I didn't make it through the program. In her effort to be supportive, Linda chose not to discuss that possibility. She knew all about my fears and insecurities because they were practically the only things I talked about during my internship. This obsessiveness, which was uncharacteristic of me, was only one manifestation of the personality transformation I was undergoing in the process of becoming a trainer.

My colleagues continually reminded me that work as a trainer is not something you do. It is a way of being that you take on with total commitment, not just in the training room but also in every aspect of your life. Becoming a trainer involved an immersion in a culture that I was unfamiliar and inexperienced with. It required a fundamental shift in my identity. This new identity required me to embody a presence that could be, depending on the circumstances, authoritative, patient, demanding, controlling, compassionate, intimidating, coercive, supportive, challenging, relentless, committed, fierce, confident, empathic, self-assured, and, often, some combination of the above.

I was in training to be an advanced course trainer, which meant that I had to be willing to be confrontational, even intimidating if necessary, and not shy away from challenges to my authority. Although being macho was never my strong suit, I set out to remake myself in the image of the senior trainers. The process of trying to contort myself into a form I didn't feel personally comfortable with was, to say the least, difficult. It also required that I take on the whole package of being a trainer. I was woefully inexperienced at the game. The "game" had to do with taking on the image and persona of a trainer: wearing the right clothes, having the right hair, driving the right car, and getting down the walk, the talk, and the look. I felt like an outsider around the other trainers, most of whom had a strongly developed sense of competitiveness, ambition, and drive, definitely the alpha males and females. About half the trainer body was made up of women.

I was well aware of how daunting the challenge was for me to fit into this new role and felt intimidated by it. I lived with a near-constant fear of failure. Failure would have meant losing not only my job but also the opportunity to fulfill what I had taken on as my life's mission. It would have meant the loss of my purpose, my dream, and all that I believed I had been born to do. It was also important, but less compelling that I had a wife at home who was taking care of our three young children, all of whom were dependent on me to provide for their needs, which required money, which required a job.

Whenever I did come home, I was often unable to deeply connect with Linda and the kids because of my obsessiveness and fatigue. Yet meaningful connection was what I needed more than anything else. The comfort of their love soothed my soul in a way that the gratification I received from work never could. But when I did two consecutive trainings—a frequent occurrence—I had less than twenty-four hours, at home before I had to hit the road again. In my rare off-weeks, I spent time with the kids to give Linda a break and keep our family intact—barely.

Adding to these competing demands, I needed some time alone. Being an introvert by nature, my tendency has always been to seek out quiet places when I feel stressed or anxious. Being alone, particularly in natural settings has always been an important way for me to find the center that I lose when I get out of balance. Although I was spending much more time away from Linda than I had ever before, very little of it was quality time alone. And because I was feeling guilty for not being there with her as much as she needed me, I tried to make it up to her by spending as much of my time and energy at home as I could. I didn't admit to myself how badly I needed time alone or how much I was affected by not getting it.

Early on in my training, Linda and I got into a pattern in which I would come home feeling depleted from having spent so much time interacting with people that I couldn't wait for some time alone, while Linda was barely able to hold on until I got home so that she could have some connection time that she desperately needed. Our needs were diametrically opposed. It was a setup for disaster, and the results often *were* disastrous.

On one such occasion, I came home three hours later than Linda had expected me to. I had stopped by the office on my way home and filled out my expense report. Two trainers were going out for a drink and invited me to join them. Against my better judgment, I agreed, adding that I only had a few minutes, if that was okay with them, I'd be happy to go. Unsurprisingly, "a few minutes" turned into an hour and a half. By the time I got home, Linda was in a fury. She raged at me, accusing me of being a rotten husband and father. She screamed that she couldn't trust me, that I didn't care about her or the children, that I was a slave to a job that sucked all my energy and time, leaving nothing for them, the people whom I claimed to love more than anyone else in the world. She admitted that she was only able to keep it together by anticipating the time when my internship would finally be over and I would be in a position to have some influence over my schedule and begin to spend more time at home.

I knew that she was right and that I had made a stupid mistake by choosing to go out with the boys, both of whom were divorced and single, rather than coming straight home. I listened to Linda, letting her blow off steam, but when I felt that she had gone on long enough and I had heard enough, I lashed out at her, using the tools I had been cultivating in the training room to accuse her of being weak and uncommitted to supporting the family and me.

"Look what kind of an example you're setting for the kids," I said, going for what I knew to be her vulnerable spot. "For once, can't you see beyond your own desires to something more important? You knew what you would be getting into when you supported me to take this job. Do you want me to quit? Is that what you're saying? Is that what would make you happy? Can't you see I'm doing my best? Do you think this is easy? What the hell do you want from me anyway?"

This was my standard tactic for dealing with Linda's increasingly frequent complaints about my lack of availability, physically and/or emotionally. I would try to let her express her disappointment and anger until I exploded. Although we were, at times, able to manage to repair our wounded feelings, her pain and disappointment, and my guilt and remorse, these breakdowns took a toll on our marriage. My strategy was to put Linda on the defensive so that the focus would not be on her dissatisfaction but on mine. Once I accomplished this, we could usually avoid Linda's feelings altogether. I had become someone who patiently gave whatever time and attention was needed to my students but rarely had enough reserves left for Linda.

During my internship I was often fearful that even if I did make it as a senior trainer, there was no guarantee that our life together would improve as much as we both were hoping it would. One way I tried to soothe Linda when she was feeling overwhelmed or drained was to reassure her that once I was promoted to a more senior position in the company, I would have more freedom and flexibility in my schedule. We both knew, however, that there was no guarantee that this would necessarily be the case. The other trainers were working full schedules, no lighter than mine. Most were unmarried or divorced, and few had children. While I told myself they had chosen to work a lot because they had nothing better to do, inwardly I feared that we were all subject to inner and outer forces that made it impossible for anyone in the training department to live a balanced life. Maybe it would never be different, and maybe none of us really wanted it to be.

There was too much at stake, however, to indulge in distracting ideas that could sap precious energy. It soon became clear to Linda that certain topics of discussion were off-limits. The consequences for violating this code were explosive outbursts from me, designed to have her keep her concerns to herself. After one of these rages, I would often feel ashamed and seek Linda's forgiveness. We would usually make up and reconnect, but despite my efforts and promises to the contrary, the cycle would continue. We were both living with the hope that it would all change when the internship was over. "Just hang in there," I kept telling Linda and myself. We lived from a shared commitment to defer the reality of our current life experience to the expectation of a happier future.

Having to unlearn almost everything that had served me in my previous career as a psychotherapist left me feeling confused and frustrated with myself. But I was usually too caught up in judgment and defensiveness to really feel these emotions, so I projected them onto Linda. Because of her relative inexperience in the trenches of emotional combat, and her willingness to absorb the heat with the hope of salvaging our marriage, she was no match for me. Whenever she would suggest that I was treating my coworkers with more dignity and respect than I was treating her and the kids, I reacted with outrage, as most bullies do. That anger was an expression of the internal rage I felt toward myself for not handling my situations both at home and at work more skillfully. Although I was being paid to teach love, personal effectiveness, and integrity, most of the time I felt like a fraud in constant danger of being discovered. Linda's accusations only reinforced my fears. Rather than listen to her, I did everything in my power to silence her, but to her credit, I was frequently unsuccessful.

Six months into my internship, I began to crack under the pressure of trying and mostly failing to keep all the plates spinning in the air. I was on my way to New York to help facilitate a workshop with Darrell, my supervisor, who was also the department head. Our relationship had never been warm. A gifted facilitator, Darrell could be intensely critical and demanding of interns and trainers. He had decided that whether I felt ready or not, the time had come for me to "jump in" and lead my first training. His purpose in working with me in New York was to provide whatever coaching I needed to be prepared to lead the following week in Calgary.

I was overcome by self-consciousness and anxiety all week. Darrell's response was to amplify his criticisms and demands, which only made things worse. On the third day of the training, Darrell said that he was leaving me in charge of the room and that he would see me at the end of the day. Three hours later he came back and, after addressing the group and sending them out on a break, gave me feedback. After leaving the room, he had stationed himself on the other side of the door and listened to what was going on. I felt undermined and humiliated, not only by his feedback but also by the sneakiness of his tactics.

I drifted back into a supportive role for the remainder of the training. On Friday I couldn't sleep and stayed up all night, giving myself permission to consider quitting. I had wanted to be a trainer more than anything else, but my heart wasn't in it. Continuing to force myself into the role would only end up causing more suffering to me, to the students, and to my family. I felt sad but also relieved. True, I didn't know what I would do for work, but somehow that wasn't an important concern now.

Darrell ran most of Saturday's training, and if he noticed that I was disengaged, he didn't show it. After we dismissed the students for the night, Darrell and I went to the hotel bar to wind down. I told him I wouldn't be going to Calgary and that I was quitting as soon as this training was over.

"Jesus Christ, what the hell is it this time?" he fumed.

I told him it just wasn't working, that I wasn't cut out for the job, and that I saw no point in drawing out the agony. For the first time, I had taken a stand during my internship. I suddenly became aware of how much I had caved to others' perspectives and of the toll this had taken on my personal integrity. I realized that one of the things I was most desperate to be free of was the requirement of subordination to the higher-ups. Darrell referred to this as my "issue with authority." Maybe so, but part of me was disgusted with the whole system and with myself for having been so compliant for so long. The elation I felt in finally taking a stand overpowered my concern over the future. I told Darrell that I was clear about my decision and that there wasn't any need to discuss it any further. We each went off to our separate rooms without saying good night.

I called Linda from the hotel, expecting her to be relieved and gratified by my decision. Instead, she said, "I don't trust that you're doing this for the right reasons. I think that you really want to be there, but you're just nervous about stepping into the lead. Maybe you're just looking for a way out."

Angrily, I accused her of not supporting me, even as I recognized some truth in her words. I hung up, and a minute later the phone rang. It was Richard. Darrell had just called him at home and informed him of my decision. Richard's tactics to talk me out of my decision were different from Darrell's. He tended to focus on establishing connections with people rather than using coercion. He could also be a skilled manipulator, but he used empathy, not intimidation. Although I hadn't always felt supported by Richard during my internship, he was the only trainer I really trusted. He asked me what had happened, and I leveled with him. I spoke for a long time while he listened intently.

When I finished, he said, "You're just scared. It's no different from what all trainers go through just before their first lead. Your mind is going wild coming up with every conceivable excuse it can find not to take this next step. And you've picked some good ones. And I'm sure that there's some truth in some of them. It's all irrelevant. "

"What do you mean?"

"Don't you see what's really at stake here? It's not so important that you continue to work for the organization. It is important whether or not you feel like a quitter. If you leave now without leading, no matter how great all your reasons and justifications are, you're going to betray something in you and confirm your own sense of inadequacy. You're up against the same kind of challenge that you've backed down from in the past, the kind of challenge that will either strengthen or weaken your sense of integrity depending upon how you respond to it. Quitting now will only deepen your doubts about yourself. I'm not saying that you can't leave; I'm just urging you to do one more training, lead Calgary, and then make the decision. Then you'll be making it from a place of strength rather than weakness, and if you do decide to go, you'll go with your head held high."

As clear as I'd been about my decision to quit, I heard the truth in Richard's words. I knew that at least part of my decision to quit had to do with taking the path of least resistance, something that I'd done more than a few times in my life. I hated to admit it, but I was suddenly open to the possibility of changing my mind. I couldn't remember ever feeling so conflicted.

Probably sensing my openness, Richard went on. "Look, I'm free next week. I could back you up in Calgary. All you need is someone that you trust to be there for you if you need them to jump in. Your problem is that you're the only one who doesn't know that you're ready to lead. The only reason that we're all pushing you to lead now is because we know that you can do this. We see it, but you don't. Look, do you think that I'd send you out there if I didn't trust your work? Believe me, you're ready."

My mind was reeling. Even though I knew there was truth in what Richard was saying, there was no way that I could see myself going to Calgary. Something inside of me was screaming to quit now and get it over with before I messed things up more than I already had. Still, I wasn't certain that I wasn't just chickening out. I told him that I needed to think it over.

At 4:30 a.m., I called Richard and told him I'd take him up on his offer. Late Monday afternoon I got home from the airport, and I'd be on my way to Calgary early the next morning. Going home for just a few hours made no sense, but I needed to connect with Linda and the kids before I took off. As I had done so many times, I leaned on Linda's love for me when I was too consumed in an orgy of self-recrimination to find even the smallest bit of confidence in myself.

I spent the short time at home with Linda getting patched up. She drove me to the airport so that we could spend a little more time together and gave me enough support to send me off feeling some degree of hopefulness. This was only one of the many times that Linda rescued me from the anguish of my inner turmoil or despair. We had developed a pattern in our marriage in which we would borrow the other's vision of us when one of us was feeling down or depressed, and find comfort in that vision and love. We came to call it "believing eyes."

For much of our relationship, it seemed that I was the one doing most of the reassuring. Although I sometimes complained about how much validation Linda needed, the truth was that I wouldn't have had it any other way. One thing I found attractive about Linda was her neediness. Something about her vulnerability was incredibly sweet. It also, of course, made her less threatening and less likely to leave me. I felt secure in her dependence, and in many subtle and not so subtle ways, I did what I could to foster it.

All that had changed in the past few months, and now I was the one in need of emotional support much more than I had been in the past. I became progressively strung out on her love and needed it at times desperately, just to get me through the day.

Comforted as we were by each other, Linda and I were locked into a pattern that provided temporary gratification at the expense of our deeper sense of integrity and self-worth. It wouldn't be until much later that we would begin to understand that love was something other than the indulging of each other's neediness. That would come with time, after much pain and struggle.

Chapter 3

I DON'T REMEMBER AGREEING TO THIS

Linda

In desperation, I had sat Charlie down for a heart-to-heart talk during one of his infrequent times at home. I was in deep despair over the direction of our lives. For me, realizing how much of a stranger he had become was a pivotal point, and I told him so in pain and anger. Looking into Charlie's eyes after fifteen years together, I said, "Who are you? I don't know you. When I see the man you've become, I don't like you much. If I met you now, I wouldn't be attracted to you. I certainly wouldn't marry you. I fell in love with a laid-back, guitar-picking hippie. Who is this guy swaggering around in a three-piece suit?"

He was spending his time building his career while I was home with the children building resentment. I thought I had chosen so carefully a man who would be steadfast and faithful to me, a man who would turn down raises and promotions to be with his family and who would be devoted to the children, a man who believed in equality of the sexes and would share power equally with me. I was stunned to see him acting like a patriarch, declaring that he knew what was best for our family. For so many years, he had been the man I envisioned, and we had made every important decision jointly. Now, in this system,

I had lost many of my rights. I had been demoted to an inferior status. How could a person change so dramatically in such a short time? The man I had fallen in love with was gone. His shadow side—aggression, ambition, greed for power, selfishness, insecurity, and fear—had taken over. I was seeing how ruthless, cold, and manipulative he could be.

How had we arrived at this low point? How had we become so estranged from each other? Ironically, it all began with the personal growth seminars. After months of involvement, we were soaring with energy and visions of possibilities. Having gotten in touch with a powerful sense of myself, I felt capable of taking the big risk to go after my own dream, to move to California to live in warm weather among people with similar values.

We experienced enthusiasm before the actual move, and the excitement of a new place carried me for the first months in California. When the elation subsided, I began to deflate. I was on my own with the children day in and day out, virtually a single parent. Whenever life was especially stressful, I told myself, "It's temporary; it isn't going to be forever." If I'd have known how long it was to last, I would have plunged into a horrible depression. Sometimes it's better that we don't know what's in store for us.

"Why the hell is a feminist like me doing all the child-rearing?" I was called upon to do more giving than I ever dreamed I would have to do. As hard as it was, the first year was actually the easiest because I was operating under the illusion that Charlie would only be unavailable to us for the duration of his training. Also, we had accumulated enough good will to have some savings in our emotional account. I was able to draw from our previously happy times. I wasn't exhausted and depleted. I was still optimistic, imagining an end in sight, when we would be a close, snug, happy family again.

Charlie was undergoing a transformation. In training to become a facilitator, he was accused of being "too soft" because he was unwilling to confront students in the way his mentor believed was necessary to break down resistance. Charlie's struggle to conform to the demands of the training department was so counter to his personality. I had always known him to be such a sweet, compassionate, and tenderhearted man.

I had keen memories of an easier time, of our meeting and falling in love. On the day we met, when he was reaching into his wallet, I saw a picture of a beautiful little girl. When I asked, he told me it was his little sister at three years old. I couldn't help but fall in love a man who carried his little sister's baby picture in his wallet. I felt my heart open with the recognition that I had met someone who was good fathering material. I remembered that in those first days, Charlie telling me about finding a mouse still alive, caught in a trap, and how he freed the mouse, fed it, nursed it back to health, and then took it to an open field to let it go. Recognizing Charlie's tender heart, I let myself fall more deeply in love.

I remembered our eight-week cross-country trip, going from one national park to another. What inexperienced campers we were at the time, fumbling to set up the tent and make the camping stove and lantern work, hiking, climbing, and swimming. Both of us gave up smoking and never went back on our vow to live a healthier lifestyle. I had such sweet memories of our honeymoon backpacking across Europe for three months. I remembered the excitement of the decision to have each of the babies, and the vivid details of each of their births were burned into my memory. Seeing how torn Charlie was between his sweet, compassionate nature and the aggressive, authoritarian style of leadership that characterized the training department was painful for me. He wasn't the only one who was feeling torn and confused. So was I.

One night, the dilemma came to a head. He had been up the whole night with a splitting migraine. I massaged his head for hours, torn between wanting to support him in his pursuit of his career and wanting him to quit. A few months later, we were up all night again, this time with pains shooting through the middle of his chest, another manifestation of the unresolved stress of trying to keep his integrity while conforming to the company's culture. His chest pains terrified me. Charlie's father had had his first heart attack at about the same age as Charlie was then. As the hours went by with no letup in the pain, I left all three children sleeping in their beds and took him to the emergency room. It turned out that he didn't have a heart problem, only pulled intercostal muscles—a result of massive stress.

Before all this, I had thoroughly enjoyed my profession as a psychotherapist. But now, I felt it would be hypocritical of me to be counseling clients about improving their lives when mine was such a mess. And I felt that the children deserved to have at least one parent present. So I let go of my life's work. It was a terrible loss to me. When Charlie's career began to take off, I felt I had trashed mine so he could be a success, and my resentment grew.

I wanted so much to have something to do for work that I studied massage and went to work in a fancy spa. It was a marked reduction in income, but I could pursue my life's work to be a healer without having to speak to anyone about anything of importance. It was essential to my self-esteem that I have some semblance of a career. Although I enjoyed practicing massage, I missed my chosen profession.

I suggested to Charlie that we have a nanny or a foreign student move in with us to assist with the housework and children. He thought it would be an invasion of our privacy. Because I remained committed to our original contract of making all major decisions by consensus, I didn't take a stand to get an au pair without his blessing. It would have made the situation much more tolerable.

My libido had always been high, and during the years from thirty-five to forty, it was soaring. Extended separations were hell. Having no access to Charlie's body and having to sleep alone most nights left me feeling terribly lonely. As a person who likes a lot of sexual contact, cuddling, and intimate talk, the separation was especially awful, even torturous. Furthermore, because so many agreements regarding rearing the children jointly and supporting each other's careers had been broken, I saw no reason why our monogamy agreement wouldn't be violated too. There were rumors about how the trainers, whether single or married, screwed around. Most of them had divorced at least once. I was both scared and angry. With morbid fantasies filling my mind, I agonized over Charlie having affairs with women in the different cities he traveled to. There were certainly plenty of opportunities. If he chose to avail himself, I knew our relationship, tattered as it was, couldn't withstand a blow of that magnitude.

I hated being a long-suffering martyr. I longed to be restored to my normal personality and to experience the loving kindness of my true self. I was so angry and resentful about feeling abandoned by Charlie that I frequently yelled at the children and was terribly critical. I found myself saying the same words I had heard as a child from my parents, words I had vowed I would never say to my kids. "Can't you be quiet for just a little while? I can't hear myself think! Stop bothering me! You are driving me nuts!" I despised myself for yelling at the kids and judged myself a bad mother. I felt Charlie's absences as rejection and concluded that I must be an inadequate wife. I felt unattractive, boring, and joyless. I couldn't compete with his exciting, glamorous career. My self-esteem was taking a terrible beating.

Perhaps for a more independent woman, it might have been fine, but the situation was extremely difficult for me to accept. I didn't have the strong supports that might have made me more accepting of it. I didn't have quality child care, and at the time I had very little personal support outside of my marriage. My close friends and relatives were on the East Coast. I had hoped that the company staff would be our community, but that was clearly not going to happen. My wanting Charlie to leave was no secret. I had never chosen to withhold my frustration and criticism of the trainers' schedule, so I was branded a company critic.

Because I was angry much of the time, Charlie ended up minimizing communication with me and devoted more time and energy to his career where he could feel successful. I didn't understand how strongly he was driven to respond to his calling. He had discovered that facilitating groups was his true gift. Some part of me knew that, and that part could support him.

But I wanted to find my own gifts too. When was I going to get my chance? This was one of the darkest periods of my life. Being alone so much of the time took me back to my childhood. I had been an only child for fourteen years until my brother's arrival and felt disconnected from my parents. Charlie was the first person I'd allowed myself to deeply trust. His absences threw me back to my original distrust. The voices of my parents kept ringing in my ears: "You can't count on anyone! People just take from you what they can get and leave." I started to slip into my old, negative thinking.

I had a vague understanding that I needed to be doing some important inner work, something about learning to be more comfortable with myself. But I fought this recognition, the very thing that would set me free. I didn't want to face the massive fear and the dark, shadowy places inside me. I didn't want to look at how many ways I felt inadequate and weak. I had serious doubts about my ability to be a competent professional woman, a loving wife, and an effective mother.

The intimacy that had been so important to me was sandwiched into five-minute phone calls from Charlie on his short dinner breaks, calling me from payphones in crowded restaurants. It seemed like his calls were duty calls. So many of them were ruined because my anger outbursts, with me yelling, "Why aren't you here? Why aren't you helping me?" And he'd say, "I can't talk now. I have to go back to the training room."

I was jealous of his students who were getting his love and attention while the children and I were relegated to second-class status. I felt victimized by Charlie, by the company he worked for, and by his boss, whom I believed exploited the employees, overworking them and separating them from their families.

Charlie's work had become "the other woman." I felt like the cast-aside wife. The exciting new mistress was the one who counted. He seemed to love her so much more than he loved me. He spent most of his time with her, and I got the leftovers. Whenever I confronted him with his job being the most important thing to him, he denied it, saying that marriage and family came ahead of career. He had been an honest man before, but this seemed to me like a complete lie.

I had never dealt with anything like this. Charlie was lost to "Mistress Corporation." No matter what I did or said, I couldn't bring him back to the family. Our situation was complicated by my coming to see the company as a kind of cult. I use the word *cult* quite intentionally because the employees and volunteers were bound together by veneration of the ideals and principles that the company espoused and loyalty to the company leader: an ideology accompanied by rituals and ceremonies and a claim of having the sole insight into understanding the problems of our times, as well as the methods to cure the malady.

To further complicate matters, I had gone through the trainings myself and had embraced the guidelines of the program. One of the main themes is to reject the identity of the victim because it is such a disempowered position. The "correct" stance, according to the company, was one of accountability: "Each of us is responsible for what we experience in life." Consequently, I blamed my weakness, inadequacy, and lack of commitment to our relationship as the sources of the growing rift between Charlie and me.

Later I became distressed by how damaging the belief that you create your own reality can be when used single-mindedly. While the principles of intention and commitment are profoundly important, these guidelines can be taken too far. I know now that I don't completely create my own reality; that is magical thinking. I am affected and influenced by other people and events. Like everyone, I am an interdependent being.

Before I saw what was really happening, I attempted to use the company's model and focus my intention and commitment on handling a situation that was actually untenable for me. When we fought, Charlie would pull out a trump card that rarely failed to shut me up. "You're uncommitted," he would say. I would resolve then to try harder to manage things in his absence. I was desperate to find the places where we were still aligned and to amplify those as much as possible in an attempt to bridge the gap widening between us. Overwhelmed by loneliness, resentment, and despair I felt trapped between my belief that I shouldn't be a victim and my feeling that I was, with no idea of how I could ever resolve this excruciating conflict.

Chapter 4

RIDING THE ROLLER COASTER

Linda

Dealing with the wide swings between my desire to make our situation work and the moments of hopelessness that so frequently possessed me was one of the most difficult challenges I've ever faced. I felt split and fragmented. Part of me loved Charlie dearly, and another part felt he was causing me unbearable pain, a part that admired the beautiful work he was doing and a part that wanted him to leave his draining job.

One of Charlie's many gifts is that he has never lost touch with his playful inner child. He is funny; everyone loves this about him. During the times he was home, he could be wonderful with the children, creative and entertaining. He often took them to the park. Although it gave me some badly needed time to myself, I spent the time catching up on tasks such as laundry and house cleaning. I was happy that he was devoted to the children, lavishing affection on them, but part of me was competitive with my kids. Longing for his attention, I badly wanted some playtime with him myself.

At bedtime, to the children's delight, he would read story after story, acting out the different characters in dramatic voices. I could hear their laughter. On one hand, I was pleased that they were enjoying each other so much, but I was also filled with such longing that it hurt. I wanted him to wrap it up with the kids and come laugh with me. Charlie has a great sense of humor. There wasn't much play or laughter in my home when I was growing up, and I was starved for the lightness that his playful rascal personality brought to me. I was charmed by his ability to draw me out of my seriousness, heaviness, responsibility, and worry. I was keenly aware of how much difference it would make for all of us if he were really available. The four of us were continually competing to get a piece of him, and there was never enough to go around.

The most dangerous time for me to fall into the well of grief was when I became overtired. As if I were four years old again, I'd find myself tumbling. It was dark and scary down there, and I felt utterly alone. Filled with despair, I didn't even have enough energy to cry out for help. It didn't seem that anyone would notice that I was missing and I didn't know if they would even care. The awful mood would pass, but it wouldn't be long before I would plummet into the depths again.

Fatigue amplified my feelings of despair. Sometimes all I had to hold on to was my commitment. My commitment to the marriage and, especially, to keeping our family together wouldn't let me quit. What I wanted most for my children was to provide the foundation of a stable family. That commitment was the glue that kept the relationship together when it was being stretched and torn. I was certain that if we'd had no children, I would not have stayed with Charlie.

My best friend listened to me cry at the ruin my marriage and family were becoming. "Leave him," she said, "You deserve better than this." I fumblingly tried to explain why I didn't leave, but I couldn't find the words to describe our connection.

I'm certainly not recommending that anyone remain in a painful situation. No one can tell you to stay or to leave. I'm just talking about my situation. Although terrible, I continued to stay. Coming back to my commitment gave me strength when I felt weak and wounded. I constantly checked in with myself to see if I could stay in a marriage that had no resemblance to what I really wanted. I knew that I would survive if I decided on separation and divorce, but I repeatedly made the choice to stay. In very dark moments, I diagnosed myself as masochistic and wondered if my self-esteem was falling so low that this was all I thought I deserved.

But then the deep love Charlie and I had for each other would emerge in a magic moment of connection that reminded me of why we were together. We designated time each week when I would set aside my anger and resentments and Charlie would set aside his preoccupation with work, and we would make a meaningful, intimate connection. We would both bring a clear intention that we wouldn't contaminate this loving time. Our talking and touching usually led to sexual communication that was deeply fulfilling. His unpleasant, arrogant, dominating macho persona would be absent during our lovemaking, and I opened up in his presence. He was always sensitive, respectful, patient, and caring. Without words, which so often sabotaged our connection, touch became the communication that bonded us.

In truth, we shared important commonalties. I was genuinely interested, fascinated really, with the work Charlie was doing. I believed in the value and power of the seminars. For a time, I, too, had been a wide-eyed zealot, proselytizing for the company and bringing in recruits. At the height of my activity in the organization, I single-handedly enrolled twenty-one new students in one course. Charlie was learning about the wizardry of being a trainer and shared with me the process of transformation he was facilitating. Without breaking confidentiality or revealing names, he described the unfolding of the students' deep inner selves, the dramatic catharsis and unloading of pain and suffering accumulated over years, the rise in self-esteem and self-confidence, and the ways in which the students supported each other.

From the very beginning of our relationship, we always had much to say to each other. We are very different in some ways, but the ways that we are alike and aligned are powerful. We both love to read, on all manner of topics, and discuss what we are learning. When we were still undergraduate students, we would meet in the library to study and then while walking home discuss ideas. All through graduate school, we continued our dialogue about how people learn, heal, grow, and maintain their gains. That fascination never dampened. After our academic education was complete, we read all the self-help books we could get our hands on. For Charlie to come home from the library with six books at a time wasn't unusual.

We did a large part of our reading in bed at night unclothed, touching skin to skin. A particularly interesting passage might stir one of us, and we had complete permission to interrupt the other's silence for discussion. For me, it was like an intellectual lovemaking, my enjoyment intense. Each of us was genuinely interested in how the other viewed reality from different perspectives. Our discussions and inquiries filled me, and the caresses soothed me. After longing all week to have his arms around me, I loved being held. I loved how he smelled, and I loved running my hands over his thick, downy body.

Our mutual passion for lifelong learning was one of the most satisfying parts of our relationship. In addition to our motivation to learn about healing and growth, we were drawn to books about how the mind works. We read and discussed books about comparative religion and spirituality. Charlie opened up a whole new world to me with his avid interest in politics. Even magazine articles offered an opportunity for lively discussion.

But once he worked for the company, we didn't have time for the reading and discussions that had so animated our life together. Charlie continued his reading on his flights to trainings. I, on the other hand, had precious few moments to get to the library and was so tired that reading a few pages was all I could muster. My days were composed of getting the kids up and dressed, lunches packed, getting them off to school, shopping, cooking, laundry, feeding them dinner, homework, baths, reading bedtime stories, and then dropping exhausted into bed, just to get up the next day to do it all again. Charlie's calls from the road were so brief, so we had no time for playing with ideas by phone. I missed our long, leisurely discussions. What took the place of these conversations was an exploration of all that Charlie was learning in the training room.

Miraculous transformations were regularly occurring in the intense pressure cooker environment created in the seminar. In the supportive, challenging, intimate environment the trainers created, people were speaking of things they had never told anyone, freeing themselves of shameful secrets. They were opening up to receive feedback from other students about how they were perceived, altering their self-perception. Students were challenged to come to terms with old pain that they had been carrying from childhood and were pressed to take full responsibility for their lives.

Our shared fascination with how people heal and grow provided a bridge for connection when we might otherwise have only moved farther apart. The biggest benefit was that I was able to enter the world where Charlie was living most of the time. By joining him in his world, I didn't feel quite so far away. In our joint understanding of what was going on for the students in the courses, we were growing together. It helped me manage my overwhelming fears that he was going ahead without me.

But still, I was terrified that he would leave me behind. His world was such a dramatic, exciting one. Mine was so ordinary and predictable; I feared being boring to him. But in those moments that I felt the significance of what transpired in the training room, I had great respect for the part that he was playing in alleviating suffering. Easing the pain of others was a joint commitment we had both dedicated our lives to years ago. In those moments, I was proud to support him in doing such important work.

When the trust was high and the communication open, we explored our personal journeys sometimes into the early hours.

Those sweet, sweet nights when we connected on all levels, intellectually investigating the truth of our own experience in terms of how people grow and develop, emotionally sharing our deepest feelings, physically holding each other, caressing, with me running the sole of my foot slowly up and down his calf while we became lost in conversation and then aroused, melting into a sexual connection before resuming the conversation—all of it lovemaking in different forms. We were transported above the ordinary concerns of our lives. And throughout the various levels of connection was woven the sense of a divine presence, bringing us ideas from a source of ancient wisdom, imparting the sacred to our sexual union, and bestowing a great blessing on us, to be at once alive and at peace.

What I was experiencing during these exquisite times was moving and profound. I didn't know how to talk about it. I was afraid people would think I was bragging or that I was too far out there with all the blessings and angels, sacred and divine. I didn't have the understanding to describe the experience. At the time, all I could say to my best friend when she advised me to leave Charlie, was, "I can't. I love him." I couldn't say, "I touch the Divine with him, and it's too beautiful and sacred to toss away, even though there is so much pain."

Then, just as suddenly as he arrived, he would be throwing his clothes in the suitcase and be off to the airport once again, a tearful goodbye, and that terrible tearing away, the ruptured life, the emptiness, and all the work of raising the children once again alone.

As long as I could feel that we were comrades, that we were on the same side, that the challenge was the difficult situation we found ourselves in, that we were no longer enemies but allies, I could keep going. When I could feel that we were sweetly connected by love, it was as if the relationship that had been moving treacherously close to dropping over the side of the precipice to destruction below moved away from the dangerous edge, and we could relax and play and live without threat for a while.

We went through this nerve-wracking process of drifting toward the edge again and again, only at the last moment becoming conscious and making the connection that kept us from falling. I stood guard over the relationship. Charlie was too preoccupied with his career to notice how much trouble we were in. My commitment to have the marriage survive and thrive kept me awake, but I wanted to be relieved of guard duty.

I was determined to make our marriage last. At the very essence of my being was an imprint handed down through the generations: to honor the family, to keep it intact. I grew up in a culture that valued the Hebrew teachings about creating a strong family unit. Yet much of what I heard growing up sounded hypocritical to me because my experience in childhood was troubled. These idealistic teachings stuck to me nonetheless.

The traditional woman in me who would do whatever she could to keep the family together was fighting with the feminist in me who kept accusing me of selling out. The inner feminist would yell, "Are you out of your mind? Any self-respecting woman would leave a man who is so neglectful and emotionally abusive. Call the divorce lawyer; you have to leave now. Don't give me that crap about how much you love the guy. I think that is a big fat excuse for being a weak coward." The traditional woman would answer, "He's doing the best that he can. He'll be back. I just need to be patient."

The part of me that ultimately prevailed was my very practical part that figured I wouldn't be much better off as a single mother with three small kids. Looking at the innocent faces of my children, I found the motivation to persevere. I held fast to the vision of what could unfold in the future if I just didn't quit.

Did I stay in the marriage because I was just too weak to leave or too frightened to go out on my own? Did I stay because I was a love addict? Did I stay because I felt unworthy of having anything better? No. I stayed because of the children, because of the connection Charlie and I were capable of, because I believed we could get through this, and because there were some important life lessons I needed to learn, and this was my crash course. I needed to become more independent and self-reliant. I needed to learn to be more loving without conditions. I needed to face my emptiness and find my own strength apart from Charlie. I can sum all this up in retrospect, but of course, at the time I couldn't see clearly at all.

An obvious question is, "Why didn't you go to see a therapist?" I considered it many times. One reason I didn't go was that I was caught in the company's negative attitudes about therapists. The prevailing view was that therapy was ineffective and reinforced people's ideas about themselves as victims. I was too frightened. With my marriage hanging by threads, I didn't dare risk seeing someone who might encourage me to snip the last shred of connection. I was only willing to share my pain with someone who I trusted to honor the sacredness of a committed marriage and the sanctity of family. I had been in the field of mental health long enough to know that many therapists encourage the breakup of marriages.

Knowing that there is no such thing as a totally objective therapist, I was too frightened to take the risk. We all bring our biases, prejudices, and life experience to each meeting with our clients. I was frightened of falling into the hands of a therapist who might reaffirm what my best friend was telling me: "Leave him. This situation is damaging you too much; it's hopeless." That was the message I was telling myself daily already. So, though I knew I needed help and frequently considered going to therapy, my fear and mistrust of myself to be able to stay in the marriage kept me away.

Knowing what I want, and having the clear vision of where I want to get to, has always been one of my strengths. Even in the early years that Charlie and I were together, I was sure about what I wanted. I knew I wanted a monogamous marriage and to have children. I was certain that as a feminist I wanted the traditional roles of males and females to shift and for us to form a real partnership to rear our children. My ideal of a committed relationship included lots of communication and real sharing. I wanted decision making to be a joint responsibility. I was clear that economic success was not my high goal; sharing and togetherness were.

Charlie came from a family of socialists who disdained capitalism, and I desired a simple family life without hard-driving career ambitions. I liked what I thought was his relaxed attitude about money and power, unlike my parents, both of whom were obsessed with the pursuit of money. Charlie was probably as shocked as I was to discover the ambitious, corporate-climbing yuppie that had been buried all those years. He loved the status and the power. He got lost in workaholism right away.

Our social life was the first area to go. We never entertained. We didn't go on family outings. We took very little time off for vacations and getaways. We didn't go on date nights. Because Charlie missed the kids so much while on the road, we stuck close to home when he was in town. I called him the "visiting dignitary."

I tried every way I could think of to pry him loose from working so much and bring him back into the marriage and family. We talked about it, and talked about it, and talked about it. Nothing budged. I raged, threw tantrums; nothing budged. I pleaded and begged. I manipulated and guilt-tripped. I threatened separation and divorce. I waited patiently for it to play itself out. I talked straight and was sweet, soft, vulnerable, and then powerful and clear in my communication. Nothing changed.

I didn't understand how a person could get lost in workaholism. I didn't realize how much of a man's ego is tied into his work and how vulnerable he can be to exploitation by a system that preys on that weakness. I was bewildered that Charlie, with the integrity and values about family life that he had before our move, could be living this way. I had no idea what I was up against.

I saw Charlie recreating a pattern from his family of origin, trying to get approval from Dad. Heads of some corporations set employees, like siblings, competing against each other, for the "blessing of the father." So many men never receive the blessing from their biological father and are starved for it. They are looking for a male authority figure to tell them that they are respected, accepted, and loved. They work horrendous schedules, sometimes killing themselves in the process trying to win that love.

So there was Charlie, a raving workaholic running after the male approval he desperately needed, and me, floundering, trying to parent three young, spirited children. The company culture promoted his workaholism, and the corporation was willing to take a man's life. If his family suffered, so be it. It is a setup for a marriage to fail. And in the end, many did.

Chapter 5

POWER STRUGGLE

Charlie

My first lead training in Calgary went well. Although I was elated at having made it through this rite of passage, I was still uncertain about my commitment and had serious doubts about meeting the requirements of the job. Not only did the demands of the training room or the work schedule concern me, but I also questioned whether I was temperamentally suited to operate as a psychological drill sergeant for fourteen hours a day. How long would it be, I wondered, before I knew whether to make this commitment?

As it turned out, it took less than a week. The next Tuesday, I was sent to Los Angeles to lead my second training. My backup trainer, Lisa, was there in a supportive role. The better I was doing, the less she needed to say. From the beginning I experienced almost overwhelming anxiety. I felt as though I was violating myself in some fundamental way. I wasn't sure whether this was just one more example of my "resistance" or whether my feelings were giving me a message that it would be irresponsible and dangerous to ignore. I shared my concerns with Lisa, who playfully teased me about not wanting to work to earn my pay this week and suggested that I ignore my feelings, focus on my commitment, get in there, and get the job done.

My efforts to lift myself up by my bootstraps were futile in the face of the deafening roar in my mind: "Get out; hang it up! You can't do this." By the middle of the third day, I had made my decision. At the beginning of a break, I said to Lisa, "Take it. It's yours. This is my last training, and this time I mean it." I had developed a reputation as the boy who cried wolf, and Lisa just laughed and said that she had wondered when I was going to quit again. I insisted that this time I was serious and that she had better take the training when the break was over because I wasn't going to. Finally, she agreed, and I spent the remaining two days mentally preparing my letter of resignation and wondering what I'd do next.

I called the office on Monday after I flew home and asked for a meeting with the president of the company and a few top staff. With the meeting scheduled for the next morning, I sat down that night and wrote a three-page letter of resignation in which I did my best to avoid blaming anybody, thanked the staff for supporting me all these months, and expressed regrets that things hadn't worked out differently. I requested that my resignation be effective immediately. Although I was glad I was quitting after and not before my first lead training, I found little consolation in it. I was filled with sadness and self-loathing. My dream would not be realized, and I was departing feeling like a complete failure. I really had wanted this job to work out, more than anything I had ever wanted, and now it was over because I couldn't pull it off.

By the time the meeting began, numbness had replaced sadness and self-recrimination. I just wanted to get things over with, then get the hell out to God knows where. By now everyone in the main office knew why we were meeting. I distributed copies of my letter and gave everyone present a few minutes to read it. This time there would be no attempt to talk me out of my decision, and for that I felt grateful. I was clear that I was finished, and I just wanted to get it all over with.

I received perfunctory thanks and the obligatory regrets. I was asked to wait in the trainers' lounge while my paycheck and termination papers were prepared. We shook hands, and I walked into the lounge in a thick haze of unreality. I just sat there and stared blankly ahead.

Darrell, who had said nothing during the meeting, came in to ask if we could go out for lunch and talk. I agreed, and he drove us to a local restaurant. He got right to the point as soon as we were seated.

"What would it take for you to stay?"

"We've been through this before," I said. "I'm finished, and that's all there is to it. I'm just not up to handling the heat of this game. It's too much for me. I gave it my best shot, but that didn't cut it."

"Don't bullshit me," he shot back. "I know you don't want to leave, and I also know that things aren't working out the way any of us want them to. So what I'm asking is how would things have to be here in order for it to work for you."

"You mean if I had a magic wand, how would I set things up for myself?"

"Exactly."

"I've told you what my problem is. I go nuts with the pressure of working on other people's timetables. Someone tells me when I'm going to lead, when I'll be ready to solo, when I'll do guest events, when I'll move to the next level. I go crazy when other people tell me what to do and when to do it, especially if I disagree. I've always been this way, and you knew it when you hired me. Maybe it's some kind of an authority issue, probably it is, but that doesn't matter now. I really tried to make it work, to not let this get in my way, but it's bigger than I am. The pressure that I feel is too much. I tried; you tried; that's the way things are set up. I don't expect you to change the system."

"So you're saying that if we took all the heat off you and let you tell us when you were ready to move up the ladder instead of our declaring the dates, then that would work for you?"

"Well, yeah, I guess so."

Darrell paused and then said, "Okay, you've got it."

"Are you serious?"

"Absolutely. You can stay a junior trainer for ten years if that's what you want. The deal is that you'll let us know when you're up for taking the next step. You'll call that shot if that's what you want. Deal?"

"It's a deal."

When I'd left the house that morning, Linda and I had both been certain that I'd come home unemployed. She was relieved by the unforeseen event of my staying, yet it seemed too good to be true. Neither of us trusted that the pressure and expectations wouldn't soon be reapplied. I'd been with the company long enough to doubt that they would change the system just to accommodate a wimp who wasn't tough enough to handle the heat.

But true to his word, Darrell backed way off and issued no more demands and deadlines. For the next three weeks, he sent me out to back up senior trainers. I told them what parts of the training I felt up to handling, and they let me take them. For the first time, I felt at ease. Rather than seeing everything I did as a test that held my future in the balance, I began to enjoy my work. It now felt exciting and challenging. With the terrible weight of the pressure now lifted, I remembered why I had initially decided to become a trainer: this was what I was meant to be doing with my life.

Three trainings later I told Darrell I was ready to lead again. The next week I led a training in Denver, and at the end of the week I knew that I had made it. I had crossed over the line. I felt confident and more self-assured than I'd ever felt in the room. The training had gone smoothly and effortlessly, and at no point did I have even the slightest doubt in my ability to handle things.

The experience felt almost magical. This was the trainer's high that I had heard so much about—that intensely compelling feeling of excitement and power. I knew that this training was a rite of passage not only in my work but also in my life. I had yearned for this sense of mastery and the feeling of aliveness and vitality. I'd never felt like this in anything else I had done. It was what I had come here to experience.

As much as I loved the thrill of feeling powerful and competent, what I found even more compelling was my conviction that I was making a real difference in the lives of a lot of people. My desire to have a positive impact on the lives of others had always been a major motivator in all the jobs that I had in my adult life. Yet as fulfilling as it had been to be a teacher, a psychotherapist, or a college instructor, those experiences paled in comparison to that of a trainer. Everything else was life-improving; but this was life-changing. Being a trainer enhanced my sense of self-worth and well-being. It released a vital life energy within me that felt vaguely familiar, like something that I had once known but had lost touch with. I now knew how to re-create it, and in no way was I ever going to lose it again.

Becoming a trainer required something of me that neither Linda nor I had anticipated. In addition to learning the technology of seminar facilitation, an essential component was the mind-set or attitude necessary for the job. As a lead trainer, my primary commitment was no longer to learn to deliver a successful training. I had already demonstrated that. It was about giving myself to "the work," absolutely and uncondi-tionally. The work was the expansion of the company because this would be needed to transform the world. Global transformation was obviously a big job that would require more trainings, more cities, and more students. To be committed meant that nothing was distracting my energy and focus from fulfilling this purpose. In the choice between work and anything else, the priority was clear.

Although I was prepared to have more expected of me once I became a lead trainer, I was not prepared for the implicit, as well as explicit, demand that I turn my life over to the company. I also was not prepared for the effect that trying to meet those demands would have on me, nor was I prepared for what it would be like to be away from Linda and the kids so much of the time. But what was an even more insidious and divisive aspect of the work was that it consumed me in a way that made it impossible for me to be with my family even when I was home. For much of the first two years I spent with the company, I struggled internally and externally with what often felt like oppressive and unattainable expectations.

What the other trainers called my "resistance" was actually an unwillingness to place work at the absolute center of my life. My colleagues attempted to support me to give up my resistance to my commitment to the work by continually encouraging me to give more fully of myself, as they were. This translated into being more of a company man and being as absorbed as they were in the concerns and affairs of the organization.

Being committed meant taking on another's concerns as your own and doing everything that you could do to assist him or her in becoming successful. In this case, the other was not a person but an organization, and supporting it to be successful was a never-ending job. Commitment meant taking yourself out of the picture, removing your ego, and surrendering fully to a higher purpose, which was worthy of your greatest efforts.

The trainers were all continually reminded of how incredibly fortunate we were to have the opportunity to serve at such a high level, to be doing such important work that clearly made a huge difference in the world. What greater privilege is there than to be able to make this kind of impact to so many lives! We were told that certain sacrifices are necessary, but that's always the case when the stakes are high. Nothing could be higher than global transformation. What kind of a person chooses the smallness of his or her own self-interests over the honor of serving at such a high level? How can anyone compare the cheap gratification of fulfilling your personal desires with the experience of being a vital participant in the process of achieving world peace? We are not simply a few people offering others the means to improve their lives. We are working for a global shift in consciousness that will bring about universal peace, abundance, and unconditional love.

At the time, I had no idea I was being subjected to an extremely effective assault on my individual identity. It never occurred to me that I was being programmed not only to believe in, but also to embody a new reality.

In my career as a therapist I had seen many examples of the consequences of putting beliefs and principles ahead of human relationships. I knew all too well how easy it is to "love humanity" but to treat the individual human beings in one's life with disrespect and even contempt.

Although I didn't realize it, what I was "resisting" was adopting this new reality. Though my objections focused more on the physical and material demands of the company, inwardly I was feeling coerced into taking on a new perceptual system, a different way of viewing myself and my relationship to my world and the people in it. Although never stated explicitly, the unspoken expectation was to prioritize the commitment to work over the commitment to family. It didn't need to be stated. We all knew it.

In the often-confusing language of the training, this concept was presented as playing a bigger game than merely supporting my family. My challenge was said to be transforming my view of family to be inclusive of the global family. By not limiting myself to a few people, I could, theoretically, be in service to the world and could continue to offer my loving support to Linda and the kids.

There was, of course, a catch: my picture, as well as my family's picture, of what loving support looked like would have to "shift," meaning that we would have to give up our views of family in favor of the company view. I was not being told that I must subjugate the needs and concerns of my marriage and family to the company or the "work." My "opportunity" was to "become big enough to own it all," that is, to be committed to having it all function, serving everyone's greater good and playing a "win–win" game.

Such artful use of jargon held out a possibility that didn't exist. I saw no way to fulfill the company's expectations without betraying my commitment to my marriage and family. Beyond a sense of responsibility, it was also a matter of what I had wanted in the experience of family.

One thing that had drawn me to Linda was the strength of her desire to create an experience of strong family connectedness. Through our family I sought the experience of wholeness that had eluded me as a child who was living in what felt like a fragmented family. Although I didn't know much about the glue that keeps such a unit together, Linda did.

My longing for family was on a collision course with my desire to fulfill my calling as a trainer. I felt the pull of these forces without seeing how my yearning for each of them could be honored and fulfilled. It seemed like a zero-sum game, a matter of one or the other. It was as if by committing incompletely to each of them I could somehow have enough to give enough to both. I didn't feel myself to be completely in either world, and so I believed the accusations of the other trainers that I lacked commitment. I was always withholding some part of me from the "work," and as Linda often reminded me, a part of me was always unavailable to her and the kids.

The more established as a lead trainer I became, the less of me there was for the family. Although I was aware that I was being pulled more deeply into the company and away from the family, the attraction to work became more compelling as my skill level as a trainer increased.

I tried to reassure Linda that the higher up in the system I went, the more involved I could be with the family since I'd have more influence over my work schedule. But all the evidence seemed to support a very different conclusion. The department heads and company executives seemed to be as consumed by their responsibilities as the trainers were, and in many cases, even more so. Unless I could somehow influence the company's modus operandi I had no real reason to believe that things would ever be different.

Was that even possible? Wasn't it my job to convince the students that they, and they alone, were responsible for and capable of creating what they most desired in their lives? If that was really true, then maybe I could, somehow, make everything work out for everyone. My job was to take the "if" out of the equation and to unconditionally commit to having that happen. In the language of the training, that would be for me, "going for the gold," the ultimate "win–win." Whether I could do that would determine the trajectory of the rest of my life.

Chapter 6

TWO WORLDS COLLIDE

Charlie

My fear that I would have to give up what I had craved for years made it hard for me to listen to Linda. Anything she said that sounded like a complaint I heard as a criticism. I wanted desperately to believe what I told the students in my trainings: that having it all is possible, that we can make things work to serve the highest good for all concerned, and that the only thing standing in the way is our fears and the belief that we're not enough. Once we overcome those, anything is possible. Although I often doubted the truth of those words when I was home, in the training room the doubt disappeared.

The Denver training had been a turning point for me in many ways. If I could fulfill a vision that just weeks before had seemed impossible, then why couldn't the same thing happen with what appeared to be another unsolvable dilemma? I thought the reason it wasn't working at home might be because both Linda and I were blinded by our limiting beliefs. I decided that if I simply committed wholly to us working it out together, we could turn things around.

Three months after Denver, Linda and I took a brief vacation without the kids, and I told her how much I wanted things to work at home and how convinced I was that we had a great chance of having that happen now that I was becoming more established at the company. I expected that Linda would be glad that she wouldn't have to worry so much, because of my reassurance. Although she did seem pleased that I was feeling more confident and secure, her response was guarded. I wanted to know why.

"The more excited that you get about your work, the more scared I get that you're going to move even further away from me and the children. It's hard for me to share your enthusiasm because I'm afraid that these changes are going to mean more separateness and it feels like there's already too much."

"But don't you see? That's what I'm saying," I said with growing impatience. "Not only do I know that I can do this work, but it's no longer going to take the same degree of obsession and energy on my part. If I could master my work challenge, there's no reason why together we can't master the one that's in front of us. Look what we're capable of when we both get behind the same commitment."

Unknowingly, I was slipping back into trainer mode, the line between professional persona and husband once again blurring. Linda had again become one of my students who needed help in detaching from the fears and limiting beliefs that kept her from being "all that she could be" and "making it all work." I was becoming so identified with my role of trainer that I brought it home and related to Linda, and sometimes even the kids, with the same demeanor and attitude that I used to manage a roomful of students. I lapsed into this role so frequently and so unconsciously that I didn't notice it, except when Linda brought it to my attention.

"Listen, I'm not one of your students, and I'm not asking you to empower me. I'm your wife, and I have feelings, whether you like them or not, and I'm asking you to listen to me now. Please don't coach me or try to get me to see things differently. I'm not interested in that. I'm only interested in being heard."

There were occasions when I could respond to Linda nondefensively, sometimes even appreciatively. This wasn't one of them. Instead, I did with her what I did with students who had the audacity to challenge my authority. I attacked, attempting to put her on the defensive by finding something in her response that I could discredit. Having spent much of the previous year developing this dubious ability, I was quite skilled in the art of verbal intimidation and manipulation, and I was not averse to using these tactics when it suited my purposes. In this instance, as in many others, my purpose was to get Linda to see things my way and to agree with me. The intent behind my efforts was not to support or empower Linda but to defeat her—to win.

My tendency to use coercion to get what I wanted from people was one that I wasn't fully conscious of and one that I tried to conceal from others. These denied aspects of myself are considered part of what is known as the "shadow," a term coined by psychoanalyst Carl Jung to refer to these hidden aspects of our personality. I was gradually becoming aware, however, that concealing my shadow didn't keep it from doing great harm in my relationships. Denying the aggressive or hostile part of my personality didn't prevent me from acting it out. In fact, it encouraged it. Such is the nature of the shadow. The more we deny it, the more we project it on to others.

A flavor of competition ran through many of my inter-actions with Linda, and this instance was no exception. It seemed I had only two ways of being with her. One was when I needed support, at which time I evoked her sympathy by expressing feelings of distress; the other was when I wanted power over her to fulfill some ego desire of my own. Both modes involved coercion and manipulation.

In this case, I wasn't interested in listening to Linda because that might mean having to reassess my conclusion, that she had no reason to be concerned about our being able to work things out. If I could get her to agree with me then she would be more at ease and would get off my back. Then I wouldn't have to deal with her complaints of neglect and disconnection.

Ironically, by openly listening, I could have created with Linda the connection that she wanted to feel at least temporarily satisfied. But my need to control and my unwillingness to feel her concern prevented me from doing so. Consequently, because Linda wasn't willing to back down either, we found ourselves once again at an impasse.

I pulled out my biggest guns, the ones I shot off when my desires were thwarted and I was angry with Linda for not accommodating me. "You're nothing but a bottomless pit of unquenchable needs that can never be filled. You're weak and self-centered! You can't stand it when I get excited or joyful about anything, and you always have to bring me down! You always have to inflict your self-pity on me because you can't stand me being happy about anything! You're not really committed to having things work out; you just want to remain dependent on me like your mother was on your father."

My assault was relentless and vicious. To her credit Linda tried to defend herself, but that only fueled my attack. She hung in there, but I refused to be open to anything that she was saying and continued my assault until we had both run out of steam. My intention was not just to get Linda to agree with my point of view; it was also to hurt her, to punish her for not accommodating me, to teach her a lesson so that she would be more willing to accommodate me when I requested or demanded compliance from her.

I was using her to vent the frustration and anger I'd felt toward those in the company to whom I was too afraid to express my anger. This was simply one example of what would, during my company tenure, be hundreds of occasions of displaced anger I dumped on Linda. This time, as in so many other instances, I was successful in inflicting damage on Linda. To her credit and to my displeasure, in this case she did not back down.

This battle, which had begun with a harmless difference of opinion, had degenerated into an abusive assault met by desperate, mainly inadequate defenses on Linda's part, all of which resulted in no resolution and only brought about more pain. Like trench warfare, in which there are tremendous losses, many casualties, and great suffering, neither side ends up with any significant gains to show for it all. The struggles just left us exhausted, diminished, and wary, not knowing when the next explosion might come or what would ignite it.

Once again, my actions had betrayed my words and revealed me to be hypocritical. Linda seemed to possess an uncanny knack for illuminating the discrepancies between my words and deeds, leaving me feeling shamed and exposed. Although I always felt like she was doing this to me, in fact, I, in my self-centered way, was taking it all personally, feeling attacked by Linda and impulsively counterattacking. My reactivity simply reinforced the vicious cycle in which we were caught.

I was so tightly in the grip of conflicting demands and expectations—mine, the company's, and Linda's—that the slightest sign of disappointment from anyone would trigger a massively defensive response. I wasn't able to defend myself and simultaneously listen to Linda, so my relationship with her was filled with frustration, misunderstanding, and missed connections.

The demands of work provided a legitimate means of avoiding conflicts. In the training room my objective was to incite the highest possible level of emotional intensity. Drama and catharsis created the appearance of depth and value in the perception of most of the students—as well as most of the trainers—and emotional expression during a training was one of the criteria that trainers used to assess its effectiveness. Although emotional intensity made for stimulating entertainment, such drama didn't necessarily translate into genuine value for the students.

The company's criterion for establishing each trainer's effectiveness, however, was different and easily measured. It came down to numbers: the number of people in the training who went on to sign up for the Success Program (SP). I was continually reminded in trainer meetings that "the only thing that tells anybody anything about the quality of your work is how many of your people go into SP."

Although SP was marketed as a program to provide ongoing support to people after they finished the Advanced Course, its primary purpose was to exploit the participants' fresh enthusiasm to bring in new enrollments. SP helped students to risk, move out of their "comfort zone," commit to their vision, and break through their "limiting beliefs." Once in the program, participants received acknowledgment and praise, from the staff and other students, for meeting their enrollment promises.

I was constantly reminded that failure to pull in acceptable numbers would jeopardize my position in the company. As solid as I was beginning to feel, I knew that I was not guaranteed permanent status as a lead trainer. Actually, no one was. None of the trainers were ever far from being "sent down," or temporarily assigned to work in a city office and relieved of their duties as a trainer. I had seen it happen to other trainers. Though such a move was ostensibly for "training purposes," it was an obvious punitive reaction designed to teach the banished trainer a lesson while simultaneously putting the rest of the trainers on notice that this could be their fate if they fell below their "quotas."

I didn't know if I was more afraid of the humiliation of being "sent down" or of the possibility of being required to work on a city staff, spending twelve hours a day on the phone trying to talk people into signing up for the training or supervising others who were doing the same thing. Although I had made it clear during my job interview that I was not willing to take any position in the company other than that of trainer, now that I was inside, I was subject to the same terms and conditions as everyone else.

The threat of being sent to a city office was only one of many tactics applied to the trainer body to keep us on our toes. Weekly meetings, which often lasted well into the night, included critical tirades against trainers whose numbers were slipping. Intense prodding, cajoling, humiliating, and threats to the "offender," often by several trainers simultaneously was spun as "support," and "feedback."

Along with sticks, various carrots motivated us. Bonuses were offered to the trainers who pulled in the, highest numbers in a quarter, Promotions and higher status were available to those who did extra work above and beyond the call of duty, and increases in pay were directly linked to our numbers. Whether it was the percentage of students in a course who went on to the next program, the number of guests the students brought to a guest event, or the number of enrollments that came from a speaking presentation, everything was measured by the same criterion: how much revenue was brought directly and indirectly into the company.

Although I didn't like or fully accept the validity of this measure I knew that I needed to play the game to survive as a trainer. I justified the necessity to buy into the company line by telling myself that operating from the dual role of facilitator and seminar marketer wasn't really diminishing my objectivity or effectiveness that much, and besides, how were we going to get on with the business of transformation if we didn't move people into SP?

Two things made it possible for me to ignore this conflict and continue my manipulative strategies. The first was rationalization. I had a carefully thought-out series of justifications for why I needed to operate this way, such as "It's for their own good," "It's really not such a bad thing that I'm doing," and "If I wasn't doing this, somebody else would and they'd be less considerate about it than I am."

The second factor that allowed me to continue manipulating the students in my classes toward my own ends was denial. Although I knew there were negative consequences to my tactics, I worked hard to deny to myself the depth of the harm I might be doing to the students and to my own integrity. I minimized to an extreme degree the damage that such manipulations cause when one who is in a position of power takes advantage of the trust that others have in him and exploits that trust for self-centered ends.

I adopted the perspective and consciousness of the department, which absolved me of guilt by making me less responsible for my actions than if I had been the only player in the game. Doing so seemed to lessen my sense of personal responsibility in the matter.

All of this was necessary to continue being a cog in the machinery with what I believed to be an exploitive system. Yet no system is perfect and the purpose that I was committed to would have to allow for some less than perfect conditions. At least this is what I told myself when the doubts kicked in. Rationalizations got me through the night but they were not without their price, which turned out to be much higher than I had ever imagined.

Chapter 7

DANGEROUS YEARS

Linda

After his rookie year, Charlie became a lead trainer, then a solo trainer, and finally a senior trainer. I was thrilled because I believed that now things would improve. But our life as a family went on much as before. He wasn't on the road less, and he wasn't less obsessed and preoccupied. On top of that, now he was arrogant.

During the early months, when he wasn't sure if he was going to make it, Charlie had humility. He asked for my support. Now he thought he was some kind of god. His ego was getting drunk and bloated on the adoration students lavished on the trainers, who were worshipped like gurus. In the training room, where he spent most of his time, he had a team of six people at his beck and call. They were constantly asking him, "Is there anything you need?" and running out to get him cups of coffee and food. He came home from the trainings with a pumped-up ego and asked, "What's for lunch?" as though I was supposed to wait on him hand and foot like his team did and worship him like his students did. I told him, "Take out the garbage."

Despite our having made real progress, there were still things that could set us back. Even during our angry interchanges, the deep love I felt for Charlie joined with a tremendous commitment to keep the family together. But the terrible fights, the stress of separation, and the fatigue from the sheer volume of work of caring for the children by myself began to wear away the substrate of love. We dangled precariously close to the edge of divorce. The angry scenes plunged me into despair and the days of recovery robbed my vitality. I just didn't know how long I could live with the fear of going over the edge.

I felt that I was in the morally superior position and that I had a hundred different ways to make me right and Charlie wrong. I'm the committed one. He's the uncommitted one. I'm the generous one; he's the selfish one. I'm the good mother; he's the neglectful father. I'm the sensitive one; he's shut down to his feelings. I'm honoring our original contract; he's breaking the contract. I'm honest; he's dishonest. I'm here devoted to the family. He's absent, making his career more important than the family, and on and on. All my characterizations had a kernel of truth to them, but to indulge in polarizing judgments just made matters worse.

I was confused about what responsibility meant in the context of our relationship. I had grown up thinking that responsibility means either taking care of somebody and doing things for them or getting them to do things. Despite my efforts to get my needs and desires met by Charlie, I was unsuccessful. Having faced so much disappointment and frustration, I was reluctant to put myself in the position of continuing to ask. In desperation, I resorted to manipulative tactics to get Charlie to feel guilty and ashamed. I was convinced that whatever I tried would activate Charlie's defensiveness and his resistance to being controlled.

My manipulation tactics included changing the subject, getting angry, intimidating him, crying, nagging, giving ultimatums, withdrawing, calling him names, being spiteful, and guilt-tripping him. Some of these behaviors are not intrinsically manipulative or negative. How I wielded them, my intention, made them manipulative. Most of the time, my intention was to get Charlie to back down and agree with me. Only occasionally was I expressing my anger with the nonmanipulative intention of clearing my feelings so that we could understand each other and connect.

I was more concerned with getting what I wanted than with considering my motivation when I went after something. I rarely thought about the consequences of getting something through manipulative means. Even when I won at the manipulation game, I lost. Whatever I received was unsatisfying because I knew that I had extorted it. The truth was that I still didn't trust that Charlie loved me or could love me. When I threatened, begged, cajoled, or threw tantrums, I usually felt guilty afterward because some part of me knew I wasn't playing fair.

One price I paid for manipulating him was that I didn't even know when I was lying to myself. One of my favorite manipulations was to play being meek, helpless, and confused. Under the stress of our living situation, I regressed into the fear that I wouldn't get the kind of nurturance and intimate connection that I wanted if I were stronger. I played it so well that I believed I was weak. I learned the art of manipulation from my mom, who was a skilled manipulator. She trained me to be a "traditional woman." She thought she was doing me a great service by bringing me up to be a quiet, unassertive, cooperative, passive woman. Still quite childlike and playing weak to attract a man and get him to take care of me. I had reached adulthood having learned my lessons well.

I didn't realize that I was playing weak and helpless and being a martyr and a guilt-tripper. In a certain sense, I was weak, but I wasn't as weak as I thought I was. I didn't know I was using tactics to get what I wanted, which was love and connection. I was doing what I thought I had to do to get that. It took me a long time to see this, and then it took even longer to replace the manipulative patterns with more direct, honest ways of relating.

I would want some love and attention from Charlie. I would want him to hold me and coo in my ear, maybe stroke my hair or rub my back. So I would drop hints: "Oh, I worked so hard today; my back aches (hint-hint)." If that didn't get his attention, I'd bring out my second approach, the guilt trip: "You never pay attention to me!"

When I began to catch myself in the act of being manipulative, I started to make real progress. When I wanted to connect, often I wouldn't say anything; I would just go over and hug him. I began reaching out to him, risking being rebuffed, and trusting that I was sturdy enough to survive if he rejected me in that particular moment. This willingness to be vulnerable is what built trust in our relationship and allowed for an intimate connection.

Charlie's manipulative style was very different from mine. He used his anger to intimidate me, and most of the time, it worked. He was loud and aggressive, and used withdrawal, coldness, and arrogance. I used to walk on eggshells a lot, always scanning to see what he wanted, in an effort to provide it, so he wouldn't explode. All his bravado was just a cover-up. While I was covering up my power, he was disguising his vulnerability.

I came to understand that I was a "stuffer" and that Charlie was an "excessive expresser." We had each found our complement. I wanted him to learn more self-restraint from me. He let whatever he thought and felt fly out of his mouth, uncensored, which hurt me. I, on the other hand, needed to learn to stop censoring so much and be more direct. As I learned to fight fairly, without stooping to manipulation and attempts to control, I became more effective in expressing my anger, and certain words dropped out of my vocabulary: *wrong, always, never, bad, failure,* and *fault.* If they crept in, I corrected myself. I found myself saying, "What works for me ...," and "What doesn't work for me ...," which kept the focus on me and didn't affix blame. And when something was said to me that did not feel true for me, I said, "That's not my experience."

At times I would be burning with anger, and knowing full well the more constructive way to express myself, I would nevertheless choose to indulge in my anger. I can remember saying, "I know if I speak right now, I'm going to blame you, and I'm going to do it anyway." At least I was conscious of my choice rather than being on automatic pilot. Later, I would learn that if I could quiet my mind, my heart knew what it wanted to say. When I spoke from this place, I felt myself standing in my own power. I felt clear, strong, and effective rather than scattered and blubbering.

When Charlie sensed my ambivalence about remaining in the marriage, he would try to back me down with his old methods of calling me overly dependent and uncommitted. But I was growing stronger. I was still very busy, working part-time and running the family virtually single-handedly, but as all three children were in school by this point, I had part of the day to myself. I had made some friends who were not involved with the company, so I was getting input about how normal people lived.

To keep from succumbing to the name-calling, I just said, "No, I'm not weak, and I'm not neurotically dependent. I value healthy interdependence, and I have a fierce commitment to this family and our marriage. That's why I've hung in there through this ordeal. I love you, and I miss you, and the children need you. And I'm not just thinking of my own well-being; I'm concerned with your health and well-being as well." And then I let it go.

As Charlie began to see that he couldn't manipulate me with his usual strategies, he gradually stopped using them. Those areas of sensitivity in me that had been my "hot buttons" couldn't be used against me anymore. The frequent, terrible fighting began to settle down. Even after our worst fights, we were both committed to somehow bringing about some degree of resolution and understanding. I was not willing to silence myself. I had to speak up about my pain and express my intense frustration. Charlie had made it clear to me years ago that he would not tolerate superficiality in our marriage. I was committed to honesty and authenticity, even though my disclosures often led to fighting. I knew that if I suffered in silence, it would destroy us. As terrified as I was by the prospect of conflict, what I was even more afraid of was living a lie.

Gradually, I learned to be less defensive. I learned to speak in "I" statements. No "you"—no blame, accusation, or telling him what to do. I learned to speak from a steady, solid place inside myself, and, most important, I learned to deliver my message and then let it go. I came to call this "going on the record," which meant I had turned my attachment to what I wanted into a preference. My compulsivity had diminished enough for me to speak without fear riddling the communication. This allowed for love to lace my message. I could experience myself as a person with dignity and grace when I spoke from my center of stillness. This style of speaking was more apt to reach Charlie without inviting his defensiveness, and I could have the satisfaction of being heard.

I realized that in the arena of job versus home, we were required to live with our irreconcilable differences. Sometimes we handled the differences with grace and sometimes with great difficulty. It seemed to me that the pain of our separations and irreconcilable differences was almost entirely mine, as Charlie was riding the wild, euphoric wave of his professional success.

After much practice, I began to delight in being able to say anything that was weighing on my heart and be heard. Being angry and upset and still being loved was tremendously freeing for me. Charlie wasn't totally repulsed, and he didn't leave me.

Free library day is a designated day when borrowers can return overdue books without fines. We instituted the policy in our relationship because, fearing reprisal from Charlie, I would withhold important information needed for the trust in our relationship to grow. I was fearful not only of his immediate angry response but also of his holding things against me and throwing grudges up to me later. We could each declare "free library day" any time we needed it.

We added new ground rules as we went along. One I added was "Don't try to fix me; just listen." I wanted to be regular people having an ordinary conversation, and Charlie would switch into trainer mode and try to fix me. I found it highly insulting. I wanted him to be present and listen as I expressed my concerns and found my own way to a solution. I felt ripped off whenever he would rush in with his "brilliant" action plan that had nothing whatsoever to do with what I wanted. His response was full of arrogance and disrespect. If he wouldn't agree with the "don't-fix-me" guideline, he wouldn't be privileged to hear about my challenges. I would only speak of these deeply intimate details of my life with him if he would listen to me and respect my feelings. I came to call this "holding my concerns with me."

I learned to dive beneath my inflamed mind to search for any fear that might be driving my emotions. Finding my fear of Charlie having an affair, falling in love with someone else, and abandoning me was easy. My rage was driven by fear. I was terrified that Charlie would have an affair. My mind kept returning to a period of estrangement we'd had in Connecticut, which had culminated in Charlie having a brief affair that nearly destroyed our marriage.

In the company, it was rumored that all the trainers, married or not, had lovers when they were on the road. I was certain that our marriage could not survive a blow of that magnitude. My attempts to control and bring my straying man back home met with fierce resistance. Accessing the fear that my children would become juvenile delinquents and grow up to be uneducated, unhappy, and irresponsible was easy.

Despite our having made real progress, things could still set us back. One of the worst fights of our life took place when Charlie was teaching a course in Honolulu. Something was particularly awful about Charlie going to romantic Hawaii without me. It bothered me a lot more than his teaching in Salt Lake City, Denver, or Washington, D.C. I had always thought we would go there to honeymoon and walk hand in hand on the beach in the moonlight. To have him there and me home with screaming kids drove me out of my mind.

This particular training was a special one, the first in Honolulu, and Charlie became so engrossed in the events of the course that he neglected to call home for several days. Our infrequent phone calls were our only connection during our separations. When we failed to have even this minimal contact, it became intolerable for me. There were various crises with the children, which I was desperate to talk over with him, and not being able to reach him was more frustrating than usual. When the course was over, he called. As soon as I heard his voice, I started to scream at him, "You're a rotten husband and a rotten father. And you're a liar. You say you care about us, but you don't. All you care about is yourself. You're a selfish pig."

Charlie tried to calm me down, but nothing he could say would appease me. I was fed up. He tried to get vulnerable with me, and I kicked him while he was down. He tried to apologize, but I would have none of it. I was in a rage and had no interest in getting over it. I was vicious and vindictive, out for blood. I absolutely did not care what I said. I normally would be receptive to Charlie's repair attempts, but this time was too little too late. I did something I had never done in my life: I slammed the phone down, hanging up on him.

When Charlie called back moments later, I did not answer.

Later that night, when I recalled the intensity of the hatred out of which I spoke, I was ashamed. I understood what had driven me to the edges of my sanity, but I was still humiliated and embarrassed to have been so cruel. When Charlie arrived home, he was afraid to kiss me hello. What really frightened me was that, for the first time, Charlie didn't reach out to embrace me. He later told me he didn't know whether I would welcome him or be enraged by his affection.

This time, when he made his next attempt to apologize for not calling for days, I was able to accept his apology and offer my own for the mean things I had said to him and for hanging up on him. We were able to patch up the damage enough to keep limping along until the next eruption.

Chapter 8

FROM BAD TO WORSE

Charlie

While there were unquestionably signs of improvement with both Linda and myself becoming more aware of our work and beginning to focus less on each other and more on ourselves, there were frequent indictors that much more work still would be required for each of our old, defensive patterns to dissolve. Although I had hoped and expected that the strains tearing at our relationship would cease after I became a lead trainer, this was not proving to be the case. In some ways, in fact, things were getting worse. During most of my first year at the company, I had been humbled by the challenge of my internship. Although I often felt anxious and inept much of the time, my need for Linda's support made me available to her in a way that allowed us to connect on a deep level. The problem was that my openness and need for Linda's support often left me feeling vulnerable and weak, and my response to those feelings was usually defensiveness or offensiveness, which often came in the form of criticism, intimidation, or blame.

For me, being dependent on Linda for support often felt painful and humiliating. Men are not supposed to lean that much on their wives. They are there to support the family, not vice versa. I considered myself a progressive, enlightened male, but deep down I was driven by some underlying beliefs that were traditional and sexist.

Much of what motivated me to take on the responsibilities of a husband and a father was a sense of duty. More to the point, I believed that by fulfilling these roles, I would earn greater respect and feel a sense of purpose and contribution in the world. I was, however, driven less by the altruistic aspects than by the desire to prop up my self-worth and by a hidden longing for power and excitement.

In the distress of that first year at the company, I had been unable to keep the walls up. I would pour out my fears and concerns to Linda, craving the warmth she provided during our connections. At times, it seemed like the only thing that got me through the day was the anticipation of our nightly phone connection.

Even as a child, I'd rarely allowed myself to lean emotionally on anyone. I'd always felt uncomfortable with those needs and either denied them or made myself wrong for having them. Needing emotional support ran counter to my image of what a man is supposed to be. Now here I was, indulging in and accepting the easy warmth of Linda's care.

The price I paid for my connection with Linda was a sense of shame and inferiority that I worked hard to conceal—a necessary price to get me through my internship. That intense suffering served to catalyze a deeply gratifying connectedness between Linda and me seemed ironic. The richness of our intimacy was fueled by the vulnerability I had rarely allowed myself before. I had never put Linda to the test as I was now, and she was unquestionably meeting the challenge. At times I was so filled with appreciation for her that all I wanted was the opportunity to return the gifts she bestowed on me.

At other times, when I was caught in the grip of fear, I saw Linda's grace as a trap that she, like other women, set to ensnare men, seducing them into the arms of the mother who really just wants to take their power and use it for her selfish ends. Within minutes, my image of Linda could transform from an all-loving saint to a vampire capable of draining my vital energies if I didn't keep her in her place. When these thoughts possessed me, the only way I could find relief from the fear of losing myself was to reestablish my dominance in the relationship. From my warped perspective, I could either be supported by Linda and be at risk of being exploited by her or be a man, which meant that I was neither dependent nor vulnerable. Thus, I would withdraw from her after I had "tanked up," as if this in some way restored me to a position of power and authority.

As trainers, we were taught that we needed to speak with absolute certainty at all times because it prevented our authority from ever being challenged or even questioned. If you don't know, then act like you do. If you speak with enough conviction, then most people won't doubt your words. "If you don't know, fake it" seemed to be the motto of the training department. This orientation fit a way of being that I had been practicing for years. The only difference was that now my posturing was socially sanctioned and even demanded by what was becoming my primary reality system, and I was getting paid for doing it! While this stance may have had its place in the training room, it was a prescription for a disaster at home.

After my breakthrough at the Denver training, there was less need for me to fake it. The good news was that I no longer doubted or questioned my ability to handle my job competently. The bad news was that the gain in confidence came at the expense of my humility, and I swung from self-doubt to arrogance in the space of a few days. In the context of the training, experiencing humility and confidence at the same time seemed impossible.

Almost simultaneously, my relationship with Linda underwent a radical change. With my diminished need for emotional support, I had less incentive to invest time and energy in our marriage. Now that work had become the source of my feelings of self-esteem and was no longer problematic for me, I embraced it with my heart and soul. This didn't leave much of me for anything or anyone else in my life. At the time, I was too busy getting high from the adrenaline and excitement of the training to be too concerned about that.

With each seminar I facilitated after Denver, I identified more with my work and grew more attached to the accompanying ego gratification. There were no more difficulties now, only challenges. And I welcomed them because each challenge brought with it the promise of a bigger high on the other side of it. I fell in love with the game.

There was, however, the small matter of the rest of my life. Now that I no longer needed Linda in the way I had before, I saw her concerns as hindrances to my desire to immerse myself in work. I viewed her emotional needs as among the challenges to overcome. Four months after I became a lead trainer, the gratitude I had felt toward her had turned into resentment, and what I had valued most about Linda, her capacity to connect deeply, I now perceived as a problematic weakness that I had to help her fix. I was convinced that I knew what was best for her, whether she did or not.

Although I outwardly believed in women's rights, my deeper beliefs about women were that they were more suited than men for the job of raising children and running the household. At the time, my view of family responsibilities was that the tasks involved were essentially mindless in nature and therefore better performed by women, because women are more temperamentally suited for the ongoing, drone-like quality of the work. That work is more congruent with a woman's "natural" predisposition toward domesticity and the fulfillment of the "nesting" instinct. I viewed family work as beneath me, being less important and requiring less intelligence, resourcefulness, and commitment than work that was done out in the "real world."

I did my best to keep these prejudices from Linda. I would often tell her how much I appreciated the work she was doing at home that was allowing me to do my work. I would tell her that her work was just as important as mine, that we were a team, that she was doing a great job, and that no one else in the world could do a better job raising our kids. What I didn't tell her was that I saw her position as subordinate to mine and of less importance.

These inner beliefs were so incongruent with the philosophy I outwardly espoused that I couldn't face the discrepancy and, consequently, lied to myself and to Linda. What I generally thought when she asked me for reassurance that I appreciated how hard she was working and what a good job she was doing was something like "If Linda was more secure within herself—like I am—she wouldn't need all this validation from me, and then she would be doing a good job and being a good mother instead of a mediocre one. Fortunately for her, she's got someone like me who can give her the kind of emotional support she needs to help her become more adept at handling her responsibilities." Although I was careful to conceal my true thoughts, they would often leak out in a condescending and patronizing tone when I spoke to her.

By the end of my second year with the company, I had become a senior trainer and was now mentoring some of the new trainees. I did two or three five-day trainings a month, putting in at least twelve hours a day. During the brief time I was home, I had little tolerance for the squabbling that seemed to be ongoing and was often angry with Linda for not being able to keep the kids quieter. While my work was deeply gratifying, I was becoming reactive to the ever-increasing level of conflict in our home.

The gap between the feelings I experienced at work and at home widened as my competence in the training room kept growing. There I felt confident, self-assured, and inspired. Staff, as well as students, treated me with a deference that bordered on reverence. My needs and desires were fulfilled as soon as they were spoken, sometimes before. At home, it was a different story.

As my frustration with our deteriorating home scene deepened, I became increasingly critical of Linda, blaming her for the way things were. Regardless of the words I chose, the underlying message was always the same: "This is your fault, your job, and it's up to you to fix it. I'm already doing my part, which is to provide the material support for the family and to coach you into being a more competent parent. Be grateful for what you're getting."

But Linda didn't seem particularly grateful for what she was getting. In fact, the more I persisted in using the coercive tactics on her that I used in the training room, the angrier and more upset she became. Underneath my efforts to help Linda, I was contemptuous of what I saw as her weakness and the jealousy that I believed made her want to ruin my success by undermining things at home. I was angry with her for being unwilling to swallow her unhappiness and play the sacrificing wife who gives up her desires for the sake of her husband. She had, after all, been doing this for years—why should she stop now? I was unable to view her experience with even the slightest bit of compassion.

As for the children, I loved them when they were happy and cooperative, now an infrequent occurrence. When they were not, I only wanted them to be quiet and stop bothering me. I wasn't able to acknowledge the pain underlying their bickering or their anger at me for abandoning them. The two biggest fears of my life were being realized, but I was too self-absorbed to notice: I was losing my marriage and my connection with my children, just like my father had—just like I promised myself I would never do.

During my second year on the job, a company-wide meeting was scheduled for the Fourth of July weekend. Staff members from cities all over the country would be flying in for three days at a plush resort in the Napa Valley. It didn't occur to me to question the decision to interfere with a holiday that we had come to look forward to as "family time." As the staff was used to working over weekends and holidays, with few days off, and few had spouses, there was no outcry over the scheduling of this meeting. One person, however, went through the roof when she found out about it: Linda.

"What's wrong with those people? How can they claim to care about families when they keep doing things like this that separate family members at times when they should be together? What kind of hypocrisy is it that drives that crazy company you work for? How can they keep putting you in the position of having to choose between your job and your family?"

For what seemed like the ten thousandth time, I was caught squirming between the two strongest forces in my life in what seemed an irreconcilable conflict. All I wanted from Linda was for her to shut up and quit adding to the stress of my life. I felt out of control and frightened of losing either of the things that gave my life meaning and security.

I saw Linda's "resistance" as the real problem, and I hated her for not being more supportive of my work. Many of the trainers made no attempt to conceal their opinion of Linda as being a self-indulgent, uncommitted, spoiled victim and unappreciative of the importance of the work to which we were all dedicated. The implicit message was that the reason I was having a problem handling it all was because I was handicapped by a shrew of a wife who wanted to control my life for her own selfish purposes and who had no understanding of the significance of what we as a company were doing. My job was to get her off her resistance and to support me, and I wasn't handling it well. Whenever it became evident that Linda and I were going through it again, the message from the other trainers, most of whom had been divorced at least once, was "Get her straight or dump her. Quit taking her bullshit."

The words of my colleagues resonated strongly with the part of me that wanted to see the ongoing conflict as Linda's fault. More than my marriage, more than my children, more than a balanced life, what I had become devoted to was staying plugged into my job. I had become a full-blown work addict.

I allowed Linda a few minutes to indulge her feelings of anger and disappointment about the Fourth of July meeting before I exploded. Out of my anger and the fear that fueled it, I launched an assault to discredit Linda's feelings and her as a person.

"You don't really give a damn about me or the work that I do, and you never have. All you care about is yourself. You think that my job in life is to make your life easy, to indulge you and treat you like the little princess that you think you are. When life isn't exactly the way that you want it to be, you whine and snivel and expect me to fix it, even if it's at my expense. You've got no real vision, no commitment to anything other than your own petty whims and desires. I've spent years trying to placate you, trying to accommodate you, trying to indulge your limitless desires and nothing helps. It doesn't do any good. You're never satisfied, and you never will be. I'm an idiot for even trying. We've got two totally different sets of values, and I don't see any way that we'll ever fit together. There's no point in us even trying to work this crap out. It's impossible; we're too different. I think it's time that we looked at calling it quits."

The words, which sounded spontaneous and sincere, were actually part of a manipulative ploy designed to intimidate Linda, to force her to see that the consequences of challenging my authority carried a high price. By upping the ante to make this about the continuation of our marriage rather than about a company meeting, I undermined Linda's view and set a new fire that required immediate attention. But this one I would fight on my terms, not hers. I knew that she wasn't willing to risk calling my bluff, even if she knew it was one. With the focus shifted to the question of the continuation of our marriage, Linda would be on the defensive, and I would be on familiar turf—in control.

Sensing my intractability, Linda backed off, as she had many times before, as I knew she would, but not before she told me how thoughtless and selfish I was to follow the dictates of such a misguided system. And not before she told me how hurt she felt that I could say such terrible things about her that we both knew were not true.

I defended myself but with less passion and drama. It wasn't necessary. The battle was over. Linda would not stand in the way of my spending three days at the meeting. As far as I was concerned, that was all that mattered. It didn't occur to me that the price being paid for my manipulations was far greater than the gratification I was receiving at work. I didn't realize that most of the accusations I had flung at Linda, about being selfish, uncaring, weak, uncommitted, and looking to others to make her happy, were projections of my own self-judgments. That I had not acknowledged, much less come to terms with, my own desire to be fulfilled and validated by others was the reason I was so reactive to this in Linda. That was also the reason I had no compassion for her, only contempt and anger. Her outrage was not only a potential obstacle in my quest for fulfillment through my work but also a reminder of my shadow side that remained blocked from my own awareness.

I wasn't open to hearing anything from Linda that could remind me that beneath the feelings of gratification that work provided me was a feeling of dis-ease that threatened to destroy the world of my dreams by exposing the dream as a nightmare. Nobody, not even Linda, was going to take my dream away from me. I had worked too hard and waited too long for it, and I wasn't going to jeopardize my position just because she wanted to spend some damn "family time" on the Fourth of July.

Linda was unhappy, but she would get over it. She would have to. My job was to help her rise to handling her situation with strength and responsibility. She would need my tough love to empower herself. One day Linda would thank me for hanging in there and seeing the potential strength in her that she couldn't yet recognize. One day the suffering and turmoil of this adjustment period would be over, and we would again be the happy family we used to be.

I was right about the recovery part. Eventually, we did find our way out of the unhappiness consuming our family. I was wrong, however, in my belief that things wouldn't get much worse before they got better.

Chapter 9

MIND ON FIRE

Linda

Charlie returned from a series of three trainings in a row and announced that he was packing up the camping gear to take Jesse fishing with another trainer and his son. Now that is a beautiful idea, fathers taking their sons to do a guy thing for five days. Under normal circumstances, I would be thrilled, but we hadn't had much contact for weeks, even by telephone, and had not fully recovered from the previous breakdowns. Charlie's mind was made up, though, and he went, promising to call from the road.

He didn't call. As it turned out, they went so far into the backwoods that there weren't any phones. Of course, I didn't know that. All I knew was that we had had practically no contact in weeks. And my resentment level was going through the roof. And now, here was another broken agreement. Finally, on the last day of the trip, Charlie called to announce that they were on their way home. With that, he put Jesse on. We talked for a few minutes, and while I was asking him to put Dad back on, Jesse hung up the phone.

This was one of those occasions when a little contact is worse than none. The conversation that had been going on in my mind for days was that Charlie didn't care a bit about my feelings, my pain, or my needs. He was a selfish bastard who didn't really love me, and I was stupid to keep on forgiving him and giving him one more chance.

Later that evening, Charlie and Jesse arrived home to find me, locked in our bedroom with a sign on the door, saying, "I hate you. Go to a hotel." We fought through the door for the next hour, with me refusing to unlock it. I screamed out my pain over feeling hopeless, neglected, unloved, and unappreciated and my anger at myself for colluding in this sick system.

Charlie tried to reason with me, explaining that they had been in such a remote area that there was no way he could call. It became a one-way fight after that. "You stupid, selfish shit," I yelled. "This relationship is all about you and what you want. Our entire life revolves around your stupid job and the company's needs. You don't consider me or my needs. You lie. You say things you don't mean. You make promises you don't keep. I can't count on you. You're never here when I need you. I might as well not have a husband at all. I have the worst of both worlds. If we were divorced, at least I could take a lover and get some attention and have two weekends a month of my own time while the children visited you."

Now it was my turn to bring out the biggest guns in the arsenal, the threat of ending the relationship. "You know we're going to end up divorced," I shouted. "You don't give a shit about me. Why don't we just get it over with, go ahead and separate, and get on with the divorce?" There was no response to my ravings.

I unleashed my meanest, lowest, smallest vindictive self. "I hate you. You're not a good husband, and you're not a good father. You're never here to fulfill those roles, and you're a fraud. You fly all over the country, telling your students how to make their lives work when yours is such a mess. You fake! You don't love me. You say you care but you don't. I'm the worn-out old shoe you toss aside. I know you're looking over your women students for an exciting new lover. I know you're going to fall in love with someone else. Let's just end it. Why prolong the agony?

"I can't live this way anymore. I can't live on crumbs. I hate living this way. I can't stand it; I hate you; I hate my life; I hate myself; I can't stand being so overwrought and irritable; I can't stand yelling at the children. I can't stand living in this tension. I can't stand waiting for you to come home. I can't stand a life of waiting. I hate being so angry so much of the time."

I kept this up until I was exhausted. I kept vomiting all the pain, grief, and rage that had been accumulating for years. Charlie didn't fight back. This time he just listened. At last, I opened the door, and I let him into the room. He held me in his arms while I wept from my sorrow of missing him, and he apologized for not calling me from the road.

After we both calmed down, we talked about what had just happened to try to understand what had caused us both to behave so badly and to hopefully learn something from this ghastly experience.

I realized that in the fight, I had demonstrated all the behaviors that don't work in a relationship. I engaged in yelling (which invites defensiveness), name-calling ("You liar; you fake"), dishonesty (telling him to leave when all I wanted was to be close to him), exaggeration (you always ..., you never ...), threat to leave the relationship (pulling the divorce card), character assassination ("You're not a good husband; you're not a good father"), telling him how he feels ("You don't love me"), not listening (I never came up for air; he couldn't get a word in), no intention to learn (not letting him speak.), attacking and blaming ("I hate you"), manipulation and guilt-tripping ("You're not a good father"), control (out-talking, out-shouting), protection and defensiveness (no vulnerability, only blame), and no acknowledgment of any fine qualities (not saying one nice thing about him). I knew better than to indulge in these unskillful tactics, but my hurt and deep fury overtook me.

Our demanding circumstances triggered our areas of sensitivity, which had lain dormant during the years we had lived a more harmonious, low-stress life. Our deepest fears were fully activated, enflaming any negotiations we attempted. I feared what I had observed in so many of my friends, couples who started out very much in love, with an idealistic vision of the future, and then when they hit the inevitable difficult betrayals and disillusionments, the breakdown turned into a breakup rather than a breakthrough.

Another of my fears was that the intensity and demands of Charlie's eighty-hour workweek would literally kill him. Heart disease ran in his family, and his father had suffered a serious heart attack before he was forty. Finally, I was afraid that his personality change would become permanent and that if he didn't leave me, I would have to leave him.

Our relationship was filled with overt fighting and covert simmering resentments that seemed even more damaging. I felt great shame about my failure as a wife and as a mother because I had unleashed so much anger and criticism at my children. I isolated myself from others to prevent these terrible parts of myself from being revealed. If I had joined a women's group or created strong friendships, I would have received support that would have allowed me to see my situation, and the company's role in it, from a different vantage point.

I was too ashamed to have people know how bad things were. My isolation kept me locked into the dysfunctional system of having only Charlie to reality test with. My sense of reality was off, but his was distorted too. Adored and worshipped by his students, he lived with the certainty that the way he saw reality was the way it was. He had the answers, and I didn't. I constantly felt diminished.

I saw myself as inferior and regarded my values about family life as small, while Charlie's grand talk of changing the world was the important work to be done. According to this view, strong desire for connection was dependent and some-what disgusting, rather than an important, basic human need. And Charlie's pompous, authoritarian, rational, threatening, aggressive tactics were a sign of strength, while my vulnerable, tender, feeling expressions showed my weakness. We became more and more polarized. I carried all the tender feelings, needs, dependency, confusion, doubt, fear, and loneliness. Charlie carried all the certainty, strength, and independence.

Charlie's qualities were those prized by the culture. When he pulled rank and used his skilled trainer tactics on me, I was usually an easy mark, and he could get me to back down. I used to say to him, "Let's be regular people." What I meant was let's be a normal husband and wife who share power. He was so identified with his role as a trainer that he couldn't let it go. From that place of inflated ego, he shamed me and I bought into it. His arrogant stance at this time was that he was too good for me and that I was lucky he stuck around. My self-esteem had fallen so low that I began to see it that way too.

I found myself longing for a simpler time before moving to the West Coast. I had experienced a period of profound healing through a weekly women's group I'd been a member of for three years. With that network of committed support, a community of friends, and therapeutic intervention, I found my self-esteem beginning to rise. Now, after having tasted the sweetness of feeling good about myself, I was once again experiencing myself as inadequate and worthless. I was afraid that I had lost all my hard-won gains and was back to square one.

The relationship, dried out from neglect, became highly inflamed. Any critical remark Charlie made could ignite a fire in my mind. He might make a simple remark like "The laundry isn't done yet," and my mind would explode with thoughts like "How dare you criticize anything around here! I slave day and night trying to hold this family together while you jet all over creation. You sired these children, but you're never here to bring them up. You don't even know where the pots and pans are in this house you've lived in for three years because you don't really live here. You live in hotels and show up here like some visiting dignitary."

Sometimes I would do a slow burn internally, and sometimes a tirade would shoot out of my mouth like a flamethrower.

We had the same fight over and over. The theme was always my accusation that Charlie had broken our contract about rearing the children together, supporting each other's career development, and being close. I was always furious about it and he was always defensive. I was fierce about wanting him to leave his all-consuming job. Charlie's commitment to his freedom and staying with the job was just as fierce.

He promised me that he would leave the company as soon as he was complete with his purpose in being there. He meant that he'd leave as soon as he had learned what he was there to learn and given what he was there to give. Charlie swore to me that he would know when that would be and that as soon as he felt it, he would leave. When I tried to pin him down about exactly when he thought that might be, he refused to put a date on it, but he asked me to trust that he did not see himself staying with the company for an indefinite future and making it a lifelong career as some of the trainers had done. His tenure there was a stage in a larger process of service, growth, and learning. He sounded sincere when he told me this, but this claim did not pacify me.

In our early years together, one of the first things Charlie became disillusioned with in me was my inability to stand up for myself. He concluded that I was weak and didn't have any self-respect because when he was angry about something, I would back down. Under the stress of our irreconcilable differences, I regressed to earlier fears. My father used anger manipulatively in my family, threatening to leave if he didn't have things his way. My mother's method of manipulating was more covert.

When anger came between Charlie and me, I felt as if I had ice water in my veins. I was panicky and frozen with the terror that someone would be physically hurt and/or emotionally devastated; then my ultimate fear would be realized: the relationship would end. No matter how trivial the issue, that is where my mind would go.

Learning to express anger was one of the most difficult things I had to learn. Not causing harm was a strong value of mine. Sometimes anger does hurt the person you are speaking to, but holding the anger back also causes harm. It can eat at the person who withholds something that needs to be honestly shared so it can be worked through.

I was terrified that my honest expression of anger would cause Charlie to leave me. I needed to reconsider the models of loving I had been carrying. The idea I held for a proper kind of wifely loving was the mushy kind. I was nurturing and caring, but what I needed to do was stand up and say, "Hey, it is unacceptable for you to do this." In our years in Connecticut, I had practiced diligently to be a worthy opponent. I had cultivated courage and learned how to assert my truth and how to stay present and not run away under attack. I had learned how to stay open and hear the pain of Charlie's communication and to admit to my complicity in the breakdown. I held on to my own truth to not give in, not to sell myself out and gloss over the problem. I had worked long and hard to recover from being anger-phobic and had enjoyed great success with my newly cultivated skills. So I was flabbergasted when all that I knew was insufficient to address the challenges we were now facing.

I feared that we were becoming so different that we were no longer a good match. Charlie had transformed from a bearded, longhaired, guitar-strumming, laid-back hippie into a hard-driving, competitive, ambitious, corporate-climbing, power-mongering workaholic in a suit. I just didn't like him much. So many of our fights were an attempt on my part to change him back into the man I had fallen in love with. He fought back by saying, "Let me be who I am. Stop trying to change me."

The story I made up was that I got the wrong partner, and I had to get rid of this one and get a new one—a tempting solution. I wanted to get away from the source of the pain, which I thought was Charlie. But when I would think seriously about divorce, my practical side would rear up immediately. I would think of the single moms I had known. Their lives were terribly difficult, and most had long periods of being alone between relationships. It is a huge challenge for a man to make a commitment to a woman with three children. I couldn't imagine anyone would want me when they met my spirited, outspoken children. Given the kind of mothering I was committed to doing, the way my kids were such a big part of my life, it seemed likely that I would be without a partner until they left home. That was thirteen years away! Divorce didn't offer a net gain.

I also feared that if I divorced Charlie, he might drift away from the children. As much as he loved them, living separately would make it harder for them to have the kind of closeness that comes from day-to-day living. I wanted my children to have their father as an integral part of their lives. I wanted them to feel his love and attention regularly. I visualized Charlie suing me for custody of the children, but I rested in the certainty that he could never win because of his work schedule. No court would see him as a fit father, away from home three weeks out of four.

I had seen enough clients who, as children, had suffered through their parents' divorce and were still dealing as adults with the impact, completely lost in the area of creating trusting, respectful, committed relationships. I wanted my kids to live in a functional family and to see up close what a healthy, wholesome, working relationship looked like. I was horrified at the idea of starting over with someone else. I didn't see anyone around me who was even a remote possibility. I was still in love with Charlie; other men paled in comparison and held no real allure. I really only wanted Charlie.

As often as I tried to psyche myself up to leave him, I just couldn't do it. I would lecture myself: "A woman who values herself, who has any self-respect at all would not live this way! You mustn't stand for it! You must take some action. Leave him!" But I couldn't do it.

I wanted to give him an ultimatum: "Either choose your job or choose me!" But I was sure he would choose his job. His issues about being controlled were so sensitive that if I used a strong-arm, aggressive maneuver, his pride was such that he would let the whole family go rather than submit. He told me that a relationship requiring him to sacrifice much of what he wanted was not a relationship worth having.

The fight when I hung the sign on the door saying, "Go to a hotel" was one of our most dangerous moments. It was the first and only time I locked Charlie out of the bedroom. I was desperate. If he had gone to a hotel, it's likely that it would have been the end of our marriage. To his credit, he didn't give up. When I finally let him speak, he talked to me through the locked door. I felt love and affection in his voice, which is why I finally opened the door. Once again, we had avoided falling over the edge. That we were in a gridlock—both of us locked in by our issues and our deepest values—was clear. Neither of us could back down.

I felt like a grieving widow left only with her sweet memories. I took them out at night to find nourishment in remembrances of happier times. But unlike the grieving widow whose husband did not choose to leave her but was taken by illness or accident, my husband did choose to leave me, again, and again, and again. It hurt every single time. The abundance of beautiful memories was overshadowed by the life I was living. The rage at his choice to keep leaving me nearly eclipsed the memories of our past.

My greatest pain came from the thought, "Charlie doesn't love me anymore." What else could explain his repeated absences? I just wasn't as important to him as I once was. I felt that I had been demoted in status from partner to housekeeper and childcare provider. His stance was "Just take care of the children and don't bother me."

Yet, there were some good days. During the weeks Charlie had off, we would sometimes pack a picnic, get the kids off to school, and go to the nearby small town of Calistoga, famous for its mineral hot springs. We would relax all morning in the hot waters, eat our picnic lunch, and be home in time to make love in the afternoon before the children got home from school.

When it was good, it was so good. These times were precious but all too few.

Charlie and I had briefly gone to marriage counseling during a difficult time on the East Coast. Despite the therapist not being particularly skilled, we still benefited because of our intention to use the hour each week for healing. Under the influence of the company and its subtle control of implied threats for violating the code, which included disparagement of therapy, we never sought the marriage counseling we so desperately needed during this crisis.

Our trust had fallen so low and we were both so raw from all the damaging fights that even if I just wanted to be close, to have a few moments of intimacy, we would quickly be embroiled in the old struggle, and what had started out as a simple request to lie down together to caress would end in a tirade: "You want me to quit my job, don't you?" I was hurt, rejected, and enraged enough to yell back, "You're right. I do want you to quit."

The overriding emotion characterizing this period in my life was loneliness. I was plagued by chronic heartache and longing. The busy activity of my days distracted me from the intensity of the desire to connect with my husband, but then evening would come. The yearning for connection became most acute after the three children were tucked into bed. Living in chronic dissatisfaction, always aching, you might think that during those years, I might get used to it. I never did. I could neither escape from nor adjust to the raw discomfort and sadness of feeling abandoned. The overwhelming desire to connect persisted.

I was so starved for sex and intimacy that I feared I would act out sexually with other men. Instead of acknowledging that fear, I projected onto Charlie. In every serious fight we had, I found myself accusing him of having an affair. A struggle was going on within me between two parts I named "Mrs. Commitment" and "Sexy Sadie." Mrs. Commitment I knew well. Sexy Sadie was becoming more powerful as the many months of neglect generated resentment.

The voice of Sexy Sadie said, "He doesn't pay any attention to you. Go find someone who will appreciate you. The selfish bastard doesn't deserve you. He's only getting what he deserves if you exchange a bit of affection with another man." I reached my lowest point when the dam of resentment burst, and for a period of a few weeks, I allowed a friendship with a man to cross my normally strict sexual boundaries. My self-esteem was so low that I needed a man to mirror to me that I was somebody, a woman with substance and attractiveness.

During those long years that Charlie worked for the company I kept waiting for his affair to happen, but it never did. It turned out to be that I was the one who transgressed our sexual boundaries. Before this, I had no idea that I was vulnerable to violating our vows of monogamy. I learned that under highly stressful circumstances, I was capable of being a betrayer myself. Although we didn't actually engage in intercourse, the extended kissing and caressing were clear transgressions of the vows of fidelity I had exchanged with Charlie. Driven by loneliness and starved for attention, slipping across the boundary line was easy. The righteous anger I felt toward Charlie allowed me to justify my actions.

I soon woke up to how I had been acting out and, truly repentant, confessed to Charlie. I offered to tell all the specifics, but he asked me to spare him the details. All he wanted to know was that it was over. I assured him that it was. I didn't dare see the other man anymore because I didn't trust myself not to cross the line again, so I excluded this friend from my life.

Years before, when Charlie had confessed his infidelity, the righteous indignation I felt was enormous. I definitely claimed the moral high ground. My stance was "How could a person be such a sleazebag to violate a sacred trust? Men, harrumph, they don't get the sacredness of the sexual act. I could never do such a thing." In the months and years after his brief affair, I did a lot of forgiving, and together we built trust. With a strong foundation, our relationship worked better than it ever had. But I still had confusion around how an infidelity could occur.

Now, ten years later, I was able to move to a greater level of understanding. I finally found out how a person could do such a thing. Ms. Self-control herself acted out sexually. With the right conditions, with enough anger, loneliness, confusion, and desperation, I could fall into another person's arms, have a sexual encounter with them, still love my partner, and still respect the sacred agreement of monogamy.

Charlie never threw my sexual misconduct up to me. He's not the kind of person to hold a grudge. He's not the jealous type. My having a sexual involvement outside the marriage has never been a hot issue for him, while for me transgressing sexual boundaries on either of our parts has been an area of great sensitivity and fear. For me, my sexual acting out signaled hitting absolute bottom. Something clicked in me, and I knew we couldn't go on this way. I didn't know what form the change would take, but this low was a turning point, the beginning of our long climb out of a horrible phase. Having frightened myself thoroughly, I knew I had to deal with the mountains of resentment. A renewed commitment to the marriage had to be coupled with a fierce commitment to my own well-being, or it wouldn't work. I started to realize how essential it is to balance commitments to self and other.

Mrs. Commitment herself was starting to think about leaving. Focusing on Charlie's lack of commitment had been preventing me from seeing my own self-doubt. As much as I loved Charlie, the demands of life married to him were beyond what I could handle. Sirens and flashing lights seemed to be going off, signaling danger, but what could I do? Who could help me?

Chapter 10

DOING MY OWN WORK

Linda

The answer to my cry for help came in the mail in the form of a flyer inviting us to a couples' workshop facilitated by Stephen and Ondrea Levine in Breitenbush, Oregon. When I called to inquire, there were two spaces left. Although it was a big commitment of time, when I asked Charlie if he was willing to go, he said yes, and I signed us up. Since we both had great respect for the facilitators, it was easy for us to open up to their message to cherish and honor each other. On a break, we asked if they had some time to spend with us privately. They offered to meet with us during the lunch break.

During our meeting I described how desperate I felt about our separations, with the children being so young. I found myself saying, "I want to dump him." My expectation that Charlie would get nailed to the wall for his irresponsibility to the family was foiled. To my surprise, I was the one who got nailed. Stephen responded, "It sounds like you are attached to your picture of what you think marriage is supposed to look like. I think some practice of nonattachment would help you." Then Ondrea spoke about the power of forgiveness meditation. The last thing I expected was to be called on the carpet when, in my mind, Charlie was the guilty party. I didn't like hearing that. Charlie seemed to be delighted by what they were saying. I waited for them to confront him, but they never did. Although I was shocked, a part of me was relieved to find out what my work was. At least now I had some sense of what I could do to help repair our marriage.

It had taken us fourteen hours to drive to Oregon. The return trip took only twelve. It felt like I dropped a heavy load of resentment and righteous indignation, which I had been carrying for years in this transformative weekend. Going to the workshop was a pivotal moment in my life. I made a commitment to a yearlong series of classes to learn about and develop a practice of mindfulness. I disciplined myself to get my attention off what Charlie was or was not doing and onto myself doing my practice of nonattachment, letting go of my picture of how the marriage should be, and practicing forgiveness. The input that I got from these two trusted facilitators gave me a focus for work to do on my own.

Doing my own work meant bringing myself back to the present moment. When I would sit in meditation, I would watch the contents of my thinking. The fear in my mind often clustered around "I don't see how I can possibly come through this ordeal with an intact family." The act of witnessing my thoughts gave me a little distance from them. By realizing that they were just thoughts passing through my mind, I saw that I didn't necessarily have to believe them. That small distance between me and my scary thoughts gave me just enough breathing room to be hopeful: "Well, maybe we could make it. There is still love there in the midst of the chaos. Maybe love will prevail."

My vivid imagination, which can easily conjure catastrophic, worst-case scenarios, created so much of my fear. My mind leaped into an imagined future in which Charlie would announce his infidelity and I knew that our marriage was completely over. The mindfulness teachings brought me back to the present moment. I could remind myself, "I am still married.

My husband makes love to only me. He returns to me after every course he teaches." When I could bring my mind back to the present moment, awareness lifted much of the heavy weight of anxiety and anger, leaving me to contend with loneliness.

The company's philosophy about commitment and intentionality had captivated my imagination, but it was such a limited life view. My exposure to Buddhist philosophy and, more specifically, Vipassana practice gave me an alternative framework for my life. The philosophy of loving kindness, compassion, nonattachment, forgiveness, and nonjudgmental awareness nourished my famished soul. As I opened to the teachings, my restlessness started to calm. My mind—on fire and full of anger and resentment—began to cool. I began to feel fortified and supported in my desire to make family harmony my greatest goal.

Learning about right effort, which is making my best attempt, was helpful to me. I acquired a way to work with my perfectionistic expectations. I could detach from the desired outcome because so many of them weren't manifesting. I soothed myself with a mantra: "We can only do the best we can do." I was acquiring a repertoire of methods to quiet myself since I could so infrequently rely on Charlie to soothe me and had few supports in the way of family and friends to help me through the dark times. While my best friend helped me hold onto some sense of myself by reflecting my good qualities, her attitude was "leave a relationship when it gets difficult." So my spiritual teachers became my main support. In my meditation class, we were taught that when your body hurts or your inner mental and emotional experience gets painful, just keep sitting there in meditation and experience whatever is present rather than getting up from your seat. I learned to keep my seat. It was a profound teaching for me not to run away from the unpleasant.

Working with the concepts of grasping and resistance, I noticed how much I was fighting what was occurring in my life, and I attempted to have less aversion. I noticed how attached I was to the way I thought things should be. I saw that I was making myself miserable by holding on so tightly. As I released my white-knuckled grip on what our family life had to look like, I began to relax at least a bit and kept my composure more. In doing so, I was more able to enjoy the little time Charlie and I did have together.

I could not help but feel overwhelming sorrow about Charlie creating a robust professional life that directly opposed my life's goals. But over time, I realized that I could restrain myself from speaking my judgments. I began to hold my sadness tenderly like a baby. Those were good days when I could contain the emotion. The more painful days were when I lost my composure and blurted out my feelings. When I was able to hold on to myself and not act out, the excessive bitter fighting diminished.

With steady, diligent practice, I gradually became more centered and less reactive—still sad and lonely but at least not swept up in fury. The spiritual practice was clearly having a beneficial effect. I had been compulsively listing Charlie's sins. They were so obvious to me. The list was long. Whenever I reflected on it, I felt helpless to stop the repetition until I learned mindfulness practice. By focusing on my breath, I could at least slow the velocity of my thought and sit quietly, allowing the deep breathing to bring the emotional arousal down.

I had to redefine strength. The strength I had been developing for years was to stand up to Charlie to negotiate for my fair share. Now that assertiveness was working against me. We were spending large segments of our precious little time together fighting. I was challenged to remember that there is great strength in surrendering. I held fast to the idea that every great warrior is wise enough to know when to surrender, repeating it countless times. "Let go" became my mantra. I sang the Beatles song "Let It Be." There were days when I could be soft, vulnerable, and open, and my efforts to surrender served me. There were other days when I relapsed and was too hurt and furious to remember what worked, and my practice of living with an open heart flew out the window. I just continued to practice, as much as I was able.

Practicing nonattachment allowed me to "have what I have" rather than wishing and hoping for something else. Forgiveness allowed me to lighten up the heavy grudges I had been carrying. The result of these practices was more compassion for my own struggle and Charlie's. We were both doing the best we could. We were both trying so hard in our own ways.

I learned from Nietzsche that "that which doesn't kill me makes me stronger." I repeated this phrase many times to myself to encourage me to keep going and to cultivate my own courage, strength, and warrior spirit. I needed all the help I could get. I wouldn't give up. I kept trying to repair my damaged sense of self. I began to work out regularly in an aerobics class to keep my body strong and to feel a sense of power in myself as a result of feeling fit. I went on meditation retreats to cultivate mindfulness and to learn how to remain centered, even in the face of huge challenges. And I began to make friends with people outside of the company.

The most important variable that allowed our knockdown, drag out fights to fade was the practical assistance from my spiritual teachers. Gradually, over many months, I began to reclaim a sense of myself. I considered my spiritual teachers my friends, mentors, and family of choice. I cut their pictures out of their flyers and kept them on the bulletin board to glance at to give me strength and inspiration to keep going.

Charlie and I kept talking and making an effort to repair our bond. Attending a personal growth workshop every season, I tried my best to implement what I learned there. I continued my reading. During those years, I hardly read a novel; I only checked out self-help books from the library. I listened to hundreds of tapes of the most evolved spiritual teachers and leaders of the personal growth movement. The work I did in workshops helped me "keep my heart open in hell," and that had a positive outcome.

Desperation over the painful predicament I was living in brought me to spiritual practice. Charlie and I were introduced to a spiritual teacher named Jack Kornfield who touched us both. In 1985, we began meeting with a small group of practitioners one night a week in Marin County. We met at a community member's home and sat and practiced together on her living room floor.

Meditation and a spiritual practice that promoted the cultivation of the warm heart of compassion were just what I needed. For the first hour, Jack and the entire group sat in silent meditation. In the second hour, Jack delivered a Dharma talk, including precepts of Buddhist philosophy with his commentary that brought the ancient wisdom teachings alive.

The mindfulness practice that we were both learning assisted me in staying more centered when I was worn out and exhausted. Cultivating the warm heart of compassion provided the balance to the teachings of the company of intentionality, responsibility, and a commitment to causing results. The missing piece for me was now found and consistently validated each Monday night: the importance of living with an open heart. The emphasis shifted from doing to being, and from causing results to not causing harm to others or self with our words or actions. I began to adopt new guidelines for living my life.

I would repeat to myself: "He's not a bad man. He's a good man who is just lost right now. I can love and hate him at the same time. I'm not a bad mother; I'm just overtired, stressed, and irritable. Any woman in my circumstances would be." I learned that making room for all the contradictory feelings was possible; I just had to grow bigger to make a space for them all.

I continued the practice of staying with what I was feeling. Being an observer helped me not be thrown off my seat when the same stressors continued. We fought less, not because I had given up or had become resigned to the difficult situation I found myself living in. I was becoming more accomplished in noticing my feelings, telling the truth about them, and not acting them out with the kinds of complaints and tantrums that characterized our early years with the company. Instead of a mind on fire, I experienced a pervasive sadness and loneliness.

Practicing forgiveness meditation, I would see Charlie's face in my mind's eye and consciously choose to bring a sense of forgiveness to dilute my strong resentment at his absences. Over and over, I listed the ways he was hurting me in the context of forgiveness: "I forgive you for not being here to help me with the children. I forgive you for making your work more important than the family. I forgive you for your angry outbursts. I forgive you for being so obsessed with your career development. I forgive you for not being here to hold me in your arms at night. I forgive you."

Sometimes it would work wonders; other times, the hurt was too dense, and the meditation couldn't reach the fury to soften it. At those times, I deteriorated into the thought pattern "I don't forgive you, you selfish asshole. The hell with you," and I would realize that I had to wait for another time and begin again. Forgiveness meditation was my main spiritual practice. After I would practice it, holding Charlie's image in my heart, I would need to send some forgiveness to myself. I would allow my face to come into my mind's eye, and then the image would sink from my forehead to my chest. I would feel myself cradled in my own heart, saying, "Linda, I forgive you for being so irritable with the children and shouting at them. I forgive you for the mistakes you are making in your fatigue. I forgive you for not being able to do anything significant with your own career right now. I forgive you for being inadequate to meet this massive challenge."

I practiced nonattachment, training my mind to focus on what we had rather than the deficiencies of our marriage and, at the same time, maintaining my vision of what I looked forward to enjoying at some point in the future. Nonattachment was some of the hardest work I had ever done.

The practice of cultivating gratitude allowed me to focus on Charlie's beauty. I learned to look through the eyes of gratitude at my beloved. I took on this practice with as fierce a commitment as I had the others. When Charlie was home, I looked right into his eyes and contacted my sincere appreciation of him. And when he was on one of his frequent trips away, I called up his image in meditation and sent loving kindness to him, listing his qualities: "He's dedicated to service in the world, he loves his family, and wants to make a contribution. He makes me laugh; he has a tender heart, and he is a good man." Each time I did the appreciation and gratitude meditation, new assets would come to me. By focusing on who he was rather than who he wasn't, I experienced more warmth and affection toward him.

I had been committed to the relationship all along, but now I recognized that what was required was for me to design a whole new scale. With these practices, my capacity to experience commitment grew. I became less reactive and had compassion for my own struggle and for Charlie's. We were both doing the best we could. We were both trying so hard in our own ways. The result was that I could create an island of sanity and intimacy in the short times that Charlie and I had together.

Even when things were deteriorating between us and resentment was simmering in me, Charlie and I continued to grope our way toward each other. Even while angry at the broken agreement to build both our careers and extreme disappointment at finding myself in a traditional marriage that we had vowed we wouldn't have, we made a connection. Instead of meeting him with my list of complaints, I prepared for reentry by deliberately setting aside my anger so that we could enjoy some time together. I came to call it "healthy denial."

The intensity of sexual desire drove us to drop the differences that strained our relationship. We were so hungry for each other physically and emotionally that we consciously chose to create an island of romantic connection even during the turbulence storming all around us. The one day a week that Charlie was home, we closed the bedroom door against the constant demands that were always waiting for our attention. We let go of the confusion about where our family was going.

For a few hours in our crazy marathon week, we were in each other's arms.

We learned over the months how to make every minute count. The limited time we had together made it that much more precious. We knew it was of utmost importance to check all judgment, anger, and resentment at the door, or the purity and sanctity of the experience would be contaminated. We were unwilling to have our precious connection time disturbed. I began to refer to this process as creating sacred time and sacred space. When we were together in this way, for a limited time my doubts about whether Charlie really loved me would be set to rest. His gentleness, tenderness, care, and respect for me were all evident and abundant during this brief interlude. These times of exquisite intimate connection reminded me of the harmony we had once enjoyed and gave me hope that one day we would consistently experience that love again.

Chapter 11

THE WOUND BECOMES THE GIFT

Linda

There is a parable about a man who wanted a well of crystal-clear water. He was rich and owned a lot of land. One day he gathered his workers together and set out for a part of his land where he thought water was likely. At a certain place, the workers began to dig. Sure enough, at ten feet, they hit water. The man was overjoyed. After three days, however, the well ran dry. He instructed his workers to dig another well in a different place. They hit water again at ten feet. Unfortunately, it had high sulfur content. The man moved on and dug another. This time the water was good, but it came in just a trickle. The man continued throughout his life going from place to place digging ten-foot wells and never really being nourished. He died disillusioned and unfulfilled. Ironically, the water the man sought was available almost anywhere he dug, but not at ten feet down. If he had only continued digging to a hundred feet, he would have found the rich, flowing stream he craved.

I first heard this story to illustrate commitment to a spiritual path, but I saw how it applied to my relationship journey. I had tried to practice, but when it got difficult, instead of staying with it, I wanted to find another way. The moral of the story is to stay with the chosen spiritual discipline and go deeply into it, the hundred-foot well. I realized that only in this way would I find the purity of satisfaction I was seeking.

I have come to understand that relationships are like this too. There are many compelling alternatives to going deeper. I felt impatient with the process, and I wanted to believe that I could have it all now. I bought into the notion that if things get too difficult or complex, the answer is to move on to someone or something else. I was tempted when things got hard in my relationship, to go dig elsewhere. But I kept coming back to my commitment and kept drilling deeper. I held fast to the story to help me stay steady and connected to my trust in the value of committed partnership.

Although life was demanding, my reactivity to my predicament lessened. I couldn't numb out to the circumstances that rubbed against the very fiber of my being, but I did use what I was learning about patience. I had been doing enough work with myself and could maintain my equanimity more easily, so we didn't fight as much. If Charlie accused me of wanting him to quit his job, I would just quietly say, "Yes, I'll be very happy when this part of your life is behind us. I think it will be good for all of us." The statement was an attempt to reassure myself. It was an affirmation that he wouldn't work there indefinitely. Charlie's response was always the same: "I'm not done yet."

We began to talk more and be closer again. We revived the tradition of having an annual honeymoon and spent a week alone without the children in Mexico. I greatly enjoyed the time that we spent being together rather than working and raising the children. We remembered why we liked each other. That week helped us keep going. After the vacation, we were able to continue to periodically steal days from the overly responsible roles of worker and parent. On those days, we could find some vision of our future together. We would be, temporarily, out of survival mode enough to see a wider picture of our life than what we were currently living.

During one of these getaways, we came up with the idea of creating a weekend workshop for couples that would incorporate some of the things we were learning about how relationships work on an optimal level. I was very motivated to do anything with Charlie since we were away from each other so often. By shifting my attention away from changing Charlie, he no longer felt smothered. He was able to approach me and, in coming closer, he said, "With all that we are learning, we could teach a great couples' course."

My heart leaped at the possibility that we might work together again. I felt that we could design and deliver a wonderful couple's course. We started right away to brainstorm ideas for the class. We both recognized immediately what the main theme of the course would be commitment. We decided to call the course "Partners in Commitment."

The adage "We teach what we need to learn" is quite true. Commitment at a much deeper level than had ever been required of us was being called for now. We immediately began the exciting process of writing the course, with challenging exercises designed to prompt the couples to a deeper level of communication—speaking from the heart, connection, appreciation for each other—ultimately culminating in a stronger commitment and their shared vision for their lives.

Given that building his career in the company was the most important thing in Charlie's life, and our relationship was the most important thing in my life, combining our main areas of interest and designing a workshop on relationships for the company made perfect sense. As a couple, Charlie and I weren't out of the woods yet, but we had learned enough that I knew we had something valuable to offer couples.

Charlie asked the company head what he thought, and we were encouraged to write the course, which premiered in Salt Lake City with thirty couples. The night before the class, I couldn't sleep because of my anxiety. In the morning, my stomach was roiling, and I couldn't get any breakfast down. "Butterflies in the stomach" is much too mild a description; my nerves were more like flying bats. Then I was afraid that I wouldn't have decent concentration because my blood sugar would be too low. I'll never forget the little bag of clothing, underwear, shoes, and stockings that I packed to take with me, being quite sure that I would be throwing up and having diarrhea before the course or on a break. I wanted to be prepared in case I had to change my clothes.

Anticipating the event was so much more difficult than the actual teaching it. Once I got started, I was able to speak, and the course was a big success. Afterward, people gave me the astonishing feedback that I seemed poised and self-assured. To me that I could be so anxiety ridden and that people out there wouldn't be able to know it was a revelation. The other huge realization was that my terror could be through the roof, but it didn't have to hold me back from doing what I was committed to doing. That first course in Salt Lake City was the beginning of a deeply fulfilling career of workshop facilitation.

I wish that I could tell you that after that first break-through, that I wasn't anxiety filled, and that I went on to teach in a self-confident way thereafter. But that wasn't how it went at all. My fear and anxiety lasted for years. During the first courses, my terror and panic eventually downgraded to anxiety and fear. But each time I got up in front of a group, I was desensitized a bit more and then a bit more. It took literally years to get to the point where I only felt excitement, not fear. Today I'm having a blast teaching, but getting there was a long haul for me.

Even though facilitating workshops was a formidable challenge, the reason that I stayed with it is because I believed in the message that I was offering to the students. I had suffered so much in my own relationship, almost divorcing from my husband on a few different occasions, to go on to develop an extraordinarily loving partnership with him. To me, when I look around at all the people who are confused, fearful, and angry in their relationships, in some ways I didn't seem to have a choice. If I didn't tell my before and after stories, I wouldn't have any peace. I believe that if we aren't busy giving our gifts, our peace of mind is limited.

All the threatening thoughts I'd had while teaching—"The people will laugh at you. They won't take you seriously. They will ask questions of you don't know the answers to, and you will look like a jerk and be humiliated. People will criticize you"—didn't come true. My fear was just temporarily hijacking my mind. In fact, the opposite of what I used to believe is true. My experience is that people are generally supportive and kind. They want you to succeed. My students gave me their caring attention and brought forth the best that I have to offer.

I'm so grateful that I found something that I was so completely committed to that it could overwhelm the immensity of the fear that I had to contend with. I know so clearly now, that fearlessness and courage do not occur in the absence of fear; they come from being committed to something that is bigger than the fear. That commitment is the one that allowed me to keep going no matter what.

The course was such a big success that we taught another one in Salt Lake City with thirty couples, and then one in Denver with fifty couples. Most important to me was the process of appreciation and gratitude that Charlie and I practiced regularly and then went on to use in the course.

In the gratitude and appreciation exercise, we searched for those things we see as beautiful in each other and verbalize them. For years, I had been starving to hear Charlie's words of appreciation; I had felt like such an impediment to him. Now the wall of resistance and resentment was coming down. I was no longer afraid to speak to him for fear of falling into an argument. I was becoming more conscious, careful, loving, and responsible. I had begun doing my own work. I realized that doing one's own work is one of the most powerful tools in life and in relation-ships. It means interrupting the patterns of blame. I was taking responsibility for my life, my fears, my mistakes, my confusion, and my unconsciousness in my relationships.

I felt that my years of holding the commitment were finally being rewarded. I was getting something that I wanted. Flying to another city, being warmly welcomed by the students there, staying in a hotel, having a break from the kids, eating in restaurants, and teaching a stimulating class were so much fun. I was delighted to have work where I could use my talent and could stretch and learn. Working with Charlie was exhilarating. Having hung in there for years, looking forward to a time when we might create something together again, I was happy.

With the Partners in Commitment seminar an immediate success, dates were set for New York and Los Angeles. Then with no warning of any kind, a letter came from the company head canceling all future Partners in Commitment seminars. No explanation was given. I was stunned. Perhaps the evaluation forms being so strongly positive and the three workshops being such a success threatened the big boss in some way. I don't know, and we never learned the reason. I felt like I had had a miscarriage. In grief over the course, I hardly got out of bed for a week.

It was the last straw for me. Prior to the cancellation, I had been able to differentiate between the value of the courses themselves and the grievances I had with the organization and the way employees were treated. I could no longer staff trainings or enroll friends. It took me months to recover from the cancellation, but what had seemed to be a great tragedy turned out to be a great blessing. The course getting the ax forced me to go independent. On my fortieth birthday, I decided that I would teach the course myself in my own hometown.

Chapter 12

LOSING IT, THEN FINDING IT

Charlie

"This job isn't good for family life" was something that I had heard from several of my colleagues on more than one occasion. I knew how true that was. Still, I wanted to "have it all." After all, wasn't that what we were telling our students? You can have it all. Just be committed to doing whatever it takes.

Those words were beginning to feel like a cliché even when I heard myself uttering them in my trainings. Yet despite my frustration, I clung to the belief that they had truth to them and that just maybe Linda and I could come to terms with the reality of our circumstances in a way that we could somehow, in some way, break the impasse in which we had been so entrenched. This hope, this belief, enabled me to hang in, despite my internal resistance to leaving my job and the external resistance from the training staff to consider leaving my marriage. The other things that allowed me to hang in there were Linda's commitment to making our marriage work and her determination to do whatever it would take to have that happen. Had she not held that stand as strongly as she did it is inconceivable that we would have made it. Although I hadn't given up, my commitment had diminished to the point where it was too weak to sustain our marriage. It was Linda's intention that got us through that difficult time.

One of the ways that her commitment manifested itself was to take responsibility for initiating events that were intended to make the best use of the little time that we had to spend together.

Later that summer Linda arranged for the two of us—no kids—to take a "honeymoon" vacation to the Yucatan Peninsula. It would be the first vacation of its kind we had taken for several years, and it was way overdue.

After being on the beach for a couple of days we started to unwind and consider the possibility of taking some of the things we were learning and putting them in a workshop for couples who were looking for answers to some of the same issues that we had been working with. "We don't have to have it all together," I told Linda. "We just have to be a little further along than the students are." While we unquestionably still had a way to go and more to learn, we had also learned a few things and been somewhat successful in implementing them in our life together.

We both were enthusiastic about this idea, especially Linda, who was still frustrated with not satisfying her desire to do fulfilling professional work. We put together a rough outline of what the two-day workshop would look like, and I presented a proposal to my supervisor, Darrell who referred me to Michael, the company president. To my surprise, he OK'd the proposal and within a few days, agreement was established with the Salt Lake office to offer a pilot program. We titled the course "Partners in Commitment" and scheduled the workshop for November.

The Salt Lake City office was excited about offering a course for couples and they easily enrolled more than enough people to fill the training room. The course was a big success. I was pleased with the results; Linda was ecstatic. The challenge and excitement of putting together and teaching the seminar together distracted Linda and me from our ongoing struggles and gave us something outside our relationship to focus on. Linda came alive with the opportunity to get back to professional work again for the first time in years. But the experience wasn't entirely blissful.

As much as she loved the work and was clearly skilled at facilitating, Linda's anxiety during our first few workshops was off the scale. She was sick to her stomach with nervousness prior to the start of each seminar and insisted on bringing at least a couple of changes of clothing in case she vomited. Having been through my own experience of stage fright, I sympathized with her and did my best to help her through a pretty serious case of nerves. Unfortunately, my efforts to be supportive often fell short of my intention. Although we were able to put most of our issues aside while we were co-facilitating, teaching together did trigger conflicts, some of which got played out in the training room. Our students witnessed live demonstrations of conflict resolution—or, in some cases, nonresolution—as Linda and I played out our power struggles. I was smart enough to not be as crude and overtly intimidating in public as I was at home, so I became subtler and more covert in my efforts to control our classes.

To her credit, Linda was beginning to stand up more effectively to me and with the confidence that came with experience, she was holding her own more and more of the time. Teaching together forced us to adopt more effective strategies for working out our differences. For one thing, having my judgments witnessed by others, particularly students, was embarrassing, and we couldn't pull off this course without practicing what we were preaching.

A second course was immediately scheduled for Salt Lake City. Within a couple of weeks, several other cities had requested a course. After completing a second Salt Lake training immediately followed by one in Denver, both of which received rave reviews, several other cities requested the course. Then, unexpectedly, the bottom fell out. I walked into the office one morning and found a memo from the company president waiting for me. It informed me that all future couples' courses were permanently cancelled—period.

I was disappointed and upset. Linda was devastated. Michael's refusal to explain his decision was just another reminder that this was his game and that if I didn't like it, well, I knew where the door was. Despite the difficulties and unresolved differences between Linda and me, the course was obviously of real value to the students, many of whom wrote very enthusiastic testimonials about their experience and wanted the course to continue. Working together had brought a higher level of trust and respect to my relationship with Linda.

Meanwhile, there were other challenges facing us. In February 1987, my career was at its pinnacle, and our family was showing the signs of the effects of years of distress. Jesse, our oldest at thirteen, had been identified as a serious behavioral problem in school, and because I was out of town so much, Linda was left with the responsibility of dealing with the messes he made in and out of school. The police had picked him up a number of times for misbehavior, truancy, and other assorted petty crimes. Around the house, he was loud, defiant, disruptive, belligerent, and increasingly out of control.

On my return from a New York training, Linda informed me that she had set up a meeting with Jesse's teacher that would include us both. I walked into that meeting feeling guilty and ashamed, knowing that a big part of what was wrong had to do with Jesse not getting the guidance and direction from me that he needed. His teacher was careful not to project blame, but as she described Jesse's difficulties to us, I knew that the hole in his life that she referred to, and that he was trying to fill, had something to do with me.

Linda and I had already signed us up to attend a couples' retreat in Santa Cruz on the following weekend. I had begrudgingly agreed, but the recent meeting with Jesse's teacher deepened my motivation to attend. The retreat would be facilitated by Barry and Joyce Vissell, a couple who specialized in couples' counseling and family therapy. Linda had been trying to get me to attend one of their workshops with her for a couple of years, but my work schedule wouldn't permit it. At least that was my excuse. The truth was that I could have rearranged my schedule, but I didn't want to. I didn't want to face how bad things were, so I allowed myself to continue being consumed by work. Having a thirty-minute meeting with Jesse's teacher was bad enough. I couldn't imagine spending two-and-a-half days telling and feeling the truth about what wasn't working in my life, my marriage, and my family. This time, I couldn't say no when Linda proposed the retreat. Part of me was very tired of running away and was terrified of where we might be headed if things didn't change. I was more terrified, in fact, about this than I was of facing the anguish and guilt I suspected were awaiting me.

On the day of the retreat we were caught in a horrendous traffic jam and ended up arriving late. Not a good beginning. Nineteen other couples were attending the workshop, and most had worked with the Vissells before. On the first night, I checked out the other participants as they offered their introductions. None looked nearly as trashed as we were. "There's no way that I'm going to spill my guts in front of these guys," I thought after about half the couples had introduced themselves. Linda apparently had other plans. She broke down in tears about twenty seconds into her opening remarks.

I was outraged and humiliated that she had exposed her pain and the horror of our situation. We had an understanding that I would not tolerate any public exposure of our problems. I insisted that my job required that I maintain an image of impeccability to the outside world and not jeopardize my credibility as a trainer. The truth was that I was terrified of being exposed as the hypocrite and fraud I felt myself to be.

I wanted to lash out at Linda and leave the room to hide my shame, but I knew that doing so would only confirm what I suspected everyone was already thinking about me. Eyes lowered, I sat silently while Linda spoke about her pain, our pain, and the children's pain. I felt judgment, anger, and pity from the rest of the room, most of which was undoubtedly me projecting my feelings. She seemed to speak for hours. Actually, it was less than ten minutes, but it felt like an eternity.

Then it was my turn. Linda's outpouring of emotion had made it impossible for me to do my usual routine of pretending that everything was fine and hiding the truth. I did my best to smooth things over without contradicting anything she had said, emphasizing the efforts that we were making to improve our situation and my sincere desire to heal the wounds. I held Linda's hand as I spoke, more for effect than out of caring for her. I was still angry with her for sharing our private business with a bunch of strangers and was upset that I now had to "clean it all up."

On Saturday afternoon, the second day of the retreat, Barry and Joyce made themselves available to couples who needed their support. We formed the group in the shape of a circle, and the facilitators invited any couple that needed help to come to the center of the room. Without hesitation, Linda raised her hand and said that we needed their assistance. I had suspected that sooner or later it was going to come to this, and I knew that I couldn't forbid Linda to speak openly about our situation because that was our intention in being there. Still, I felt shame, anger, and dread as I had the night before with Linda's exposure of our problems to the group. This time, however, we were really going to take the plunge, and, as she looked at me with tears in her eyes and extended her hand for me to join her in the center of the circle, I felt a kind of terror that I had never felt before.

Heart racing, I took her hand and we walked into the middle of the circle. We sat opposite each other. Joyce sat next to Linda and Barry sat next to me. They motioned the rest of the group to move in closer to the center of the room, and I felt like we were enclosed in a secure, but claustrophobic embrace. My fear began to diminish in the presence of the sense of support that I was starting to feel. As it did, deep sadness filled me. I struggled to resist the tears, biting my lower lip and clenching my muscles. Not a word had yet been spoken.

After what felt like an eternity, Linda was invited to speak. In between sobs, she spoke of the pain she was feeling, how much she missed me, how much the kids needed me, and how much she had wanted to be strong enough to raise the kids without me and to manage things at home. She spoke of her disappointment in herself, how angry she was that she wasn't strong enough to make it all work, and what being stretched so thin for years was doing to her.

She spoke of her helplessness in giving the children the kind of guidance and strength they needed and of the fear she saw that underlay Jesse's pervasive hostility. "They need you. We all need you. Please, Charlie, you have to understand. I'm doing my best; I can't do any more. It's just not working."

I choked down my emotions, determined not to be manipulated by what I assessed as Linda's drama, and reacted with my standard response: "I know that you're doing your best, and I know that it's hard. We're all trying and we've got to keep trying. We both know that if we stick with this and stay committed, it's going to work out. What do you want me to do, quit my job? Is that what you want? Do you think that's the answer? We've got to find a way to make this work."

I was putting out my standard rap, trying to turn Linda around one more time. But this time it was different. Barry stopped me. "Look at her," he gently urged. "Just look at her." Linda was sobbing out of control now. I wanted to bolt out of the room. I wanted her to stop it. I hated her for making me feel guilty and humiliated, and I felt trapped. My insides were churning, but I was still keeping it together. "I'm not going to fall apart," I promised myself.

Joyce touched my arm and spoke of the enormous love she felt between Linda and me and how deeply feeling we both were. Her words sounded as though they were coming from someplace far away and inside myself at the same time. As she spoke, I found my emotional walls crumbling and the armor around my heart melting. I looked into Linda's tear-filled eyes and for the first time saw the true depth of her love. I also saw her pain. I saw Eben's pain and Jesse's pain and Sarah's pain, as though for the first time. I saw the deep suffering that underlay all the fighting and abusiveness that we had been living in for so long. I saw the depth of everyone's sadness and unfulfilled longings, and I was filled with anguish. I collapsed into deep sobs that wracked my body. I lost my breath. I couldn't speak. I lost all the control that for years had kept my act together, and I broke down and howled like a baby.

I felt arms around me, and hands holding and caressing me. Someone said something about *my* pain, and I instantly dropped another ten stories. In that moment, I realized that it wasn't just about Linda and the kids missing their connection with me; it was about what I had missed with them. I saw what I had missed in my absences and in the years of disconnection. I saw the experiences that had come and gone that I would never have with them.

I saw Jesse's Little League games, Eben's soccer matches, and Sarah's dance recitals that I'd missed. I saw the birthday parties I hadn't attended, the meals we didn't share, the camping trips we didn't take, the cuddling in bed we didn't do, the comfort I didn't provide when the kids were scared and hurt, the homework help I was too busy or tired or absent to give, and the games we didn't play together. I saw it all and it was all too much. The grief felt bottomless. The anger, rage, guilt, fear, and desires were all gone. Everything was gone except endless sadness and irretrievable loss. It wasn't just Linda and the kids who had lost; it was all of us. I hadn't seen that before.

In the space of a moment, it seemed I was seeing all that I had succeeded in denying for the past five years, and I experienced what felt like a lifetime of sorrow.

There was no comforting me. Nothing anyone could do or say could take away the horror of what I was seeing and feeling. Linda and I held each other and cried together as one. There were no words and no need for them. I don't know how long it went on, but at some point, the tears stopped, and I looked into her eyes, oblivious to the forty people around us. Two words came out of my mouth from a place I didn't know. "It's over," I told Linda that the nightmare was finished, forever. We cried together some more.

We held each other while Barry and Joyce spoke to us and to the group about the healing power of shared love and beauty of our open hearts. They invited other participants to share their feelings with us. Linda and I let go of each other and turned and faced the group. As I listened to their words, I no longer felt shame and embarrassment, instead, what I felt coming from them was great respect and caring. I needed to do or say nothing. I just listened and took in the support. I was grateful and felt my heart overflowing, this time with love and gratitude instead of grief and sadness. I couldn't believe how quickly and dramatically my inner experience had changed. My head was spinning.

Suddenly, as if I had just remembered something I had forgotten, I turned to Linda and said aloud, as if we were alone, "I wonder what we're going to do."

"What do you mean?" she said.

"I have no idea what I'm going to do for work now. All I know is that I've got to quit my job."

"I'm not sure what we're going to do either," Linda responded, "but we'll come up with something. We can make it work because we're together now, really together, for the first time in a long, long time. We'll do it. The hardest part is behind us."

I felt the depth of Linda's support and her commitment to working as partners carrying the weight of the responsibilities we would be challenged to meet in new, as yet, unknown ways. I wasn't alone. I no longer had to feel like I had to carry it all myself. It also felt more than a little scary because I wasn't certain that the worst of our ordeal really was behind us.

In a way, Linda was right. In a way, she wasn't. For her, the worst was over. For me, it was about to begin.

Chapter 13

RESTORING TRUST

Linda

At the end of the Vissells' workshop I was laughing and crying at the same time, overwhelmed by joy that the worst was truly over and that Charlie was coming back to the family. My greatest wish was coming true. Finally, he understood what I had been trying to tell him for so long. He was now making the choice to put family first. It had taken forty people joined together in a room with a caring and fierce intention to reach him, but he was, at long last, ready to let go of the company. I felt immense gratitude toward the facilitators and every single student in the class who had supported me and opened Charlie's heart and mind. With great sincerity, I thanked them all.

The day after the workshop, Charlie turned in his resignation. In the days that followed, my doubts began to creep back in. Charlie had attempted to resign before, and his supervisor and the big boss had always been able to reel him back. I feared that they would be able to manipulate him again and that he would believe that there was no way outside the company to serve on such a grand level.

As the weeks passed and Charlie's last day on the job neared,

I became increasingly more anxious about finances because the income we were generating was not enough to cover our expenses, and I could see no other possibilities on the horizon. Charlie didn't seem to be very concerned, but I knew that he was. Then just before Charlie's last scheduled training, he was offered the option of working for the company as a contract trainer doing one training a month as an outside consultant. As much as we would have loved to have spent the next few months making up for lost time, that was a luxury we could ill afford. The company's offer seemed like a gift from heaven.

I responded to the news with mixed feelings, concerned that it was just another way to hook Charlie into coming back to the company: "They're trying to keep you connected, and then pretty soon you'll find yourself making exceptions to the one-training-a-month agreement, and before you know it you'll be back to the same craziness that you just got out of." I asked him to promise me that he would, under no circumstances, agree to do more than one training in any given month.

My skepticism caught Charlie off guard. Although I could see what a godsend this offer was, I still didn't trust that he wouldn't get hooked. I didn't trust that he had learned his lesson. Charlie reacted to my concern with hostility and defensiveness, the way he always did when he perceived me as threatening his grip on something he very much wanted. He yelled at me for not trusting him and hurled a few insults for good measure and to make sure I got the message that if I wasn't going to respond the way he wanted, then I was going to pay. In what seemed like no time at all, we were both reminded that those old, reactive patterns hadn't gone anywhere simply because he had was leaving his job.

Charlie apologized to me and expressed deep remorse over how quickly his defensiveness had come up. Charlie told me that his outburst left him shocked and deeply disturbed, but I wasn't all that surprised. I knew that it was going to take a lot more than a change in his career for us to establish a new equilibrium in our marriage. I knew that we were both feeling lost and insecure. I recognized Charlie's aggression and coerciveness as an effort to maintain the pretense that he was standing on solid ground.

I had come far enough to see his reaction as his fear of losing our much-needed income as well as confusion about what his next career would be. Even though there was a wise decision made, there was still grief in severing his association with the company that had been such a huge part of his life for years.

I feared being a contract trainer would be the beginning of him sliding back into the company, based on witnessing slides that other trainers had made. Hard as it was to get into the training department, it seemed even harder to leave it. Of the trainers who had quit over the years, the vast majority had returned. Some had been through the cycle several times. The prevailing mythology about leaving was "You always come back."

I had good reason to be fearful. Charlie had not gotten his lust for the juice of the training room out of his system. It wasn't simply that the work was exciting and challenging and filled an empty place in his life; it went way beyond that. Charlie had reported to me numerous times that in no other place and under no other conditions had he ever felt so whole and complete. His position as a trainer was what he had been waiting his whole life to find. I couldn't be sure that what we would create together would give him this feeling.

Despite my reservations and our upset because I expressed my distrust, Charlie held fast to his commitment to one week of training a month. As a few months passed, my confidence grew that we had escaped the clutches of the company. I began to think, "The worst is over; let the healing begin."

We started putting our family back together and getting our new couples' course on the road. What bliss to work together and to have Charlie back home so much of the time. I marveled at how quickly the desert that had been my life bloomed once it was watered. While I was growing and building my capacity to hold pain without being swept away by it, unbeknownst to me, I was also becoming more able to experience joy. So when Charlie left his consuming job, my gratitude and pleasure in being reunited with him multiplied. We were reestablishing ourselves as a real family. We had the great gift of time to take the kids to the park to play, to go on hikes, and to read them bedtime stories. We were parenting the children jointly, doing housework, talking through issues, and making collaborative decisions. There was sufficient cash coming in during those six months, so we didn't have to worry about money.

I relished the time our family spent together, savoring each conversation, each touch, and each shared meal. I was no longer grumpy with the children, no longer a whiner and complainer about my lonely life, no longer exhausted from raising the three kids alone. I was in a good mood most of the time, and the arguments stopped. I marveled at how quickly we were recovering.

We did a lot of repair work. Charlie and I engaged in long conversations, trying to understand what had happened to us that distorted our judgment during those years with the company. I searched for the lessons in the experience. I admitted that my desire for a community of people who were committed to personal growth and planetary transformation had blinded me. By the time I realized the nature of the organization, we were already deeply entangled and couldn't get out. As we each admitted to our parts in the breakdown, the entire atmosphere in the house changed. Our passion for personal growth coupled with idealism had made us easy targets for an organization that claimed to have "the Answer."

During the one week a month that Charlie was still conducting training sessions, I began to appreciate how this schedule allowed me to be myself apart from him. I came to see the importance of our learning to enjoy being apart from each other. I didn't learn anything at all from my family of origin about being apart, much less handling it well. My parents were joined at the hip. Neither went anywhere without the other.

My model of a close, loving relationship was one in which

the pair were in each other's face all the time. Interdependence had not been my strong suit. Charlie was the complete opposite in this area. He came from a family in which everyone did their own thing. People even ate different meals, at different times, in different rooms. In my family, we were so enmeshed that members literally ate off each other's plates. When Charlie and I were first together and I reached over to take a morsel from his plate, I got a small stab to my hand with his fork. It was a playful yet meaningful gesture; I got the message that he didn't play that way.

Charlie is private and protective of his own space and independence. At the beginning of our relationship, I took this personally. I've always wanted lots of connection; he's always wanted lots of space. The harder I pursued him, the more he withdrew from me, which caused me to feel more insecure and unloved, which, in turn, activated my desire to reconnect. This was the vicious cycle that we had been locked in and were now struggling to break.

While Charlie was doing his work of softening his strict, private, independent boundaries, I was working at establishing boundaries and independence. Part of this work consisted of loosening my attachment to Charlie and creating a life of my own. Before this, the only time in my life in which I felt truly happy was when Charlie and I were deeply connected. I spent most of the rest of the time waiting for him and that closeness.

Breaking our codependent ties was some of the hardest work I've ever done. I increased contact with my women friends and developed my career. I spent a lot of time apart from Charlie. By holding onto it so tightly, I had been squeezing the life out of our relationship. In acknowledging my own strength, I no longer believed that he alone had saved me.

When Charlie was fully present with me our intimate connection was fulfilling. When I felt full, I was able to wish him well in whatever his interests and activities were at the time. Our separateness allowed him to feel his own desire to be close to me. I was overjoyed to hear Charlie say, "We need to sit down and talk something over." For years, I had always been the one that initiated that sort of conversation. Other words that filled me with joy were "Would you like to lie down on the bed together for a while?" Charlie knew what my favorite thing in the whole world was.

Intimacy has always been the part of a relationship that comes easiest to me. I have always been in touch with my longing to connect, and open to giving and receiving love. Anger and confrontation were more difficult for me. I had to learn how to be comfortable with all of it. Being alone has always been hard for me. I wanted marriage to protect me from feeling lonely. I can see clearly now that much of the giving and loving I did in the early years of our marriage was tainted. It wasn't really giving; it was investing. The cooking, touching, sweet talk, and some of the sexual contact were efforts to bind Charlie to me by bribing him with a variety of gifts.

I came to the relationship looking for love, unable to access it within myself. The implicit deal I had struck was "I'll give you the love and nurturance you are craving, and you take care of me." When Charlie became a trainer I felt betrayed, as though he had violated our contract, yet there was a clause in our original marital vows that we would always honor change. In the process of rebuilding our trust, I began to see the bigger picture, and slowly but surely I was able to see the experience not just as a horrible thing that I had to live through but also as an indicator that our relationship was maturing. We were both growing in self-sufficiency and autonomy, and that was a good thing!

As we each took responsibility for our contribution to the deterioration of the relationship, the trust began to deepen. Instead of seeing myself as having been a victim of a selfish, work-addicted husband, I began to look at the positive elements of the experience. Instead of seeing Charlie as having left me, I reframed the dramatic changes as part of the evolution of our marriage.

I came to appreciate our separations and see them as a gift

that had been given to us. When I was on my own, I was forced to reach down and find resources I hadn't known were there. Yes, it had been a painful time, and I had hated it. If I hadn't been so enmeshed in our relationship, the tearing wouldn't have been so painful. Out of the ordeal grew a strength and wisdom, and I began to learn how to take care of myself. I began to honor my interests apart from family: friends, career development, and spiritual life. Without this initiation by fire, I would not have reached this point.

I came to appreciate that couples do need to be apart from each other at times. It is when we are separate that we can look inside to see who we are and what we need. It is so easy to get distracted by those we love, and we can veil our truth by tuning into the needs of others to the exclusion of our own. The more I learned about allowing my children to be who they are, the stronger and more loving they became. The more control I was able to let go of in my marriage, the more we could thrive. We moved from a fear-based relationship to a love-based relationship.

What had kept our relationship closed to input and stimulation from the larger world was my fear of loss and abandonment. Spending time separately allowed us to miss each other, and to experience passionate reunions. New things to learn, new ideas, and new possibilities became available.

As I saw that I could let go and not lose our connection, I began to go off on trips too, both for work and fun. Being apart while maintaining emotional connection became a revitalization process. I noticed some couples around me, who, after years of being together, were experiencing a sense of stagnation because their lives had become routine and predictable. I was grateful that our relationship was thriving. We were growing as individuals, learning new things, meeting new people, and deepening our connections with old friends. I could see how much we were bringing to each other after reuniting after a separation. I could now view our periodic times apart as a sign of health for us. What allowed our time apart to be wholesome rather than destructive was a high level of trust. I could finally relax into knowing that Charlie and I were both committed to doing what would enhance our relationship.

It was at this point that I heard a story about a king who owned a large, pure diamond of which he was justly proud. One day, the diamond accidentally sustained a deep scratch. The king called in the most skilled diamond cutters and offered a reward to anyone who could remove the imperfection from his treasured jewel. But no one could repair the blemish. The king was sorely distressed.

After some time, a gifted lapidary came to the king and promised to make the rare diamond even more beautiful than it had been before the mishap. The king was impressed by his confidence and entrusted the precious stone to his care. The man kept his word. With superb artistry he engraved a lovely rosebud around the imperfection, using the scratch to form the stem.

The story became a reminder to me to trust Charlie and myself. We used the deep gash on the diamond of our relationship to create a work of art even more beautiful than it had been before. I was amazed at how only months earlier, our marriage had been in shambles, characterized by a slow burn of resentment, angry outbursts, and a chronic undertone of resignation on my part. While I was steeped in hopelessness and frustration, it seemed as if it would take years to pull out of the destruction, if indeed we were to ever pull out of it at all. Instead, our badly damaged trust was quickly making a recovery!

Chapter 14

FREE AT LAST

Charlie

The day after the couples' retreat, I walked into Michael's office and for the third time in four years tendered my resignation. Uncertain of where I was going in my career, I was clear about one thing: this time it would be final.

We exchanged some small talk, but Michael knew that something was up. When I told him of my decision, he seemed surprised. Before I even got to the point of my meeting with him he interrupted me with thinly disguised anger, impatiently asking, "What is it now?"

Michael had been under the impression that I had not been unhappy with my work situation, which was mostly true. Though I thought it would be better not to try to explain my reason for leaving, I tried anyway and soon realized that I was attempting to justify my decision, to get him to understand, even agree with it. Not surprisingly, I failed miserably.

Though part of me felt flattered in knowing that I was valued by the company, the rest of me couldn't take pleasure in that because I felt now that I had nothing to be proud of. The feelings of shame and remorse that had been activated just days earlier at the retreat were still burning within me and what I most wanted to do was to get on the track of my new commitment ASAP. For once, Michael's approval meant nothing to me. I didn't care how badly he wanted me to stay or even how he felt toward me. I was hurting too much for that. I just wanted out.

My two previous resignations had given him reason not to take me seriously. In the past, I hadn't really wanted to quit; I wanted things to change in ways that were more to my liking. When I was finished explaining myself, Michael came back with the question, "Okay, so what's it going to take for you to stay? Is it more money you want, more time off, what is it?" There was impatience in his voice, as though he was tired of having to deal with my "special needs."

"No, Michael, this time it's different. There's nothing you can offer me now to make this work. It's not about more money or time. It's just not working for me anymore. I'm tired of being on the road so much, tired of being gone from my family all the time. It's really wearing thin for all of us, and I've got to get out and go home. I'm just done."

I told him that although I was giving notice, I was willing to stay on to complete the trainings that I was scheduled to lead. The schedule had been made out until the end of April, another seven weeks. This would give me a chance to make my transition out of the company a little more gradually, and it would give the training department time to do whatever reorganizing or hiring might be necessary to maintain coverage in the interim between my announcement and my actual departure from the company.

Michael accepted my resignation and told me that my tenure with the company would end May 1. I left feeling incredibly relieved. For the first time in ages, I felt something other than anguish: a sense of hopefulness that this termination might transform into a new beginning. Although outwardly nothing in my life had changed, inwardly things seemed completely different. Though I would still be doing trainings, at least for the next two months, and had the same problems and concerns waiting for me at home with Linda and the kids, the same unpaid bills, the same squabbles and arguments, none of it felt the same.

I was no longer running away from it all. I could see the finish line from where I was. And although there had been some damage and injuries that had been sustained, there would soon be time to make repairs and put things back together again. Freed of the weight of the relentless demands of my work, I experienced an almost euphoric sense of freedom and peacefulness. I began to realize just how burdened I had been without knowing it. No wonder I always felt so tired and put upon when Linda wanted anything from me. Yes, I had managed to master my craft and had been excited and challenged along the way, but at what price?

I was disturbed by my capacity for self-deceit. No wonder things had gotten so bad at home and I had gotten so out of touch with Linda and the kids. I was so hungry to succeed in my work that I had blinded myself to anything that could possibly interfere with it. I began to see the extent of the damage my blindness had caused. There was too much to take in all at once. It came to me in bits and pieces, but even in small doses the remorse and guilt that accompanied these realizations were very painful, more painful than I cared to experience. "It was awful," I told myself." "Thank God it's over, and I've learned my lessons and can put the nightmare behind me."

The same denial that had kept me from seeing the extent to which my work addiction had been damaging all our lives told me now that the worst was over and things were on the upswing. I wanted to believe that I had handled things during the retreat and that there really was very little for me to do now beyond implementing a few changes at home and generating some income. I assumed that since I had both the time and Linda's support, there was no reason why this challenge couldn't easily be met. Sure, things had gone somewhat to hell, but now that I was able to see and understand the problem, all that was history—except that as it turned out, it wasn't.

I was following the formula of the training room: denial, confrontation with the truth, cathartic breakdown, awakening, and breakthrough to a new reality. I had seen it work for students. It would work for me. After all, I had fulfilled all the requirements for transformation, and now all that remained was to implement the necessary changes. As far as I was concerned, my training was pretty much over. I had "gotten it." It was a hard lesson, but I was sure that the degree of pain in the catharsis corresponded to the value of the lesson, so I was grateful to have such a powerful teaching behind me. It had been a close call.

We had pushed things pretty far, almost too far, and some serious prices had been paid. But Linda and I were fortunate. We had broken the cycle in the nick of time and were spared the possibility of having our marriage and family decimated, and now we would go on. Not only was I convinced of this, but Linda was as well. As it turned out we were both mistaken.

I hadn't yet begun the process of recovery from what I now see as my work addiction. I was like an alcoholic who was about to give up the bottle but hadn't yet found a healthy substitute for it. In the meantime, there was work to be done, much of which required my willingness to finally listen to the concerns that Linda had been trying to get me to hear for the past five years, much of which I had deflected or ignored.

When I finally was willing to listen to her concerns as something other than personal attacks or attempts to control me, I recognized their validity. Once again, Linda had seen something that my own blindness had caused me to miss: the legitimate danger of going back into the belly of the beast and the need to take certain precautions and set certain limits to keep from being swallowed up again. Though I now knew my physical and emotional health, as well as the well-being of the family, depended on me staying unplugged from the training circuit, the prospect of letting go of the work left me feeling anxious. I was the moth irresistibly drawn toward the destructive flame.

Although it was clearly time for me to move on, I was deeply afraid of losing the source of my connection with the sense of purpose and the feelings of exhilaration that I experienced in the training room. I feared that without that, life would be empty and hollow. I knew of no other way of re-creating that feeling outside of the training room. Unless those deeper needs could be fulfilled in nonaddictive ways, I feared that I would be at risk of joining the others who had been caught in the cycle of leaving the company and returning.

As it got closer to my termination date, Linda and I became increasingly concerned about replacing the income my salary had been providing. I had been looking into other work possibilities, but nothing was panning out, largely, I suspect, because I was unrecovered from the burnout that I had been experiencing.

In mid-April Michael called me into his office and offered to hire me as a part-time consultant who would do one training a month. He offered enough money to take the edge off our financial concerns. I hadn't considered that this could even be possible. All the trainers were full-time employees and hiring of an outside contract trainer had no precedent.

Accepting Michael's offer would not only cover our basic expenses, but it would also give me and Linda time to promote and enroll the couples' workshops that we had begun to market in different cities throughout the country. It was a no-brainer. I tried not to seem too exuberant in response to Michael's offer, but failed miserably. My enthusiastic "Yes!" betrayed the cool composure that I was trying to maintain.

The terms of the contract were that I would have no administrative or supervisory responsibilities and would not be required to attend trainer meetings. I would have a degree of autonomy previously unheard of in the company. Between the income, the opportunity Linda and I would have to promote our courses and build our business, and the time I'd have available for kids, it was the best of both worlds and seemed almost too good to be true.

Relieved of the enrollment pressure and the demand to upgrade students, I felt free and creative in a way I hadn't been before. After completing my first contract training, I felt rested and energized. Because I didn't have to attend the trainers' meeting being held the following day, I could go straight home from the airport. And I wasn't scheduled to go back into the training room for four more weeks!

That summer and fall were probably the best months our family had experienced since our move to California. We had time to be together, Linda and I were scheduling and facilitating our own workshops in several cities and our network was rapidly growing. For the first time in years, we were beginning to feel like a family again. We were, however, very far from having put the pieces back together.

But things continued feeling strained and difficult with the kids. They were still attacking each other, either verbally or physically, with Sarah, the youngest, often the target of her older brothers' angry impulses. She, in turn, knew how to provoke the boys, prompting harsh responses to them from Linda or me. Capitalizing on her position as a victim, Sarah got back at her brothers through us and deepened the anger amongst them.

Linda and I were aware that the kids were simply mirroring what they observed as the way to handle painful emotions. I experienced each of the children's cries as an indictment of my failure as a father to provide them with their most basic needs: a loving, supportive family in which they felt safe and cherished. No longer able to escape to work and having to spend so much of my time at home, I was confronted with the anguish that left me feeling the full impact of my neglect. Sarah, like her mother, was the wounded victim who was powerless against the males in her life by whom she felt controlled. Unable to assert herself honestly and directly in the face of their power, she was becoming manipulative, self-pitying, calculating, and covert.

The boys, having failed to see an example of male vulnerability, learned to do exactly what they had observed in me: transform their pain and fear into anger, which they projected onto others and acted out in destructive behavior. Like their dad, they, particularly Jesse, were learning to use anger to intimidate others and as a shield to protect them from feeling the softer, more threatening emotions that lived below the surface. The more frustrated I became at being unable to remove these disturbing symptoms from our family environment the more they persisted. And how could they not? What Linda and I failed to see at the time was that we hadn't shown the kids any other way of responding and that they had no other options in their behavioral repertoire.

Yet despite our frustration and anguish, we remained hopeful. We reassured each other that as difficult as witnessing and listening to the ongoing conflicts between the kids, surely things would calm down after a time and harmony would once again be restored to the family. We had made the changes and taken the necessary steps in the process of bringing about healing the hearts of our wounded family. Of course, it would take time, but we were on the right track, doing what needed to be done. That was the main thing. We just had to be patient, we told ourselves.

After six months, Michael informed me that he was terminating the contract at the end of the year. It was causing too many problems among the other trainers, many of whom were now asking for similar arrangements. I had a choice: either I could come back to the company as a full-time trainer or I could find another job. I wasn't surprised. I had known the contract wasn't going to last forever. I thanked him for giving me the option to return and respectfully declined his offer.

I was anxious about the loss of a good chunk of regular monthly income but confident that Linda and I would make things work out. The couples' workshops were going well. We had facilitated several of them in different cities and been invited to return to do more seminars. We had a small following of people who supported our work and who were willing to set up and enroll future courses for us. As long as we could keep things moving this way, we'd be fine.

I did my last contract training in Washington, D.C., the week before Christmas. Not surprisingly I left with mixed feelings. Although I felt good about what I had accomplished and learned during my tenure at the company, I felt some disappointment over not having experienced the degree of camaraderie that I hoped to feel with the trainer body.

I never did make it fully into the inner circle of this small band of idealists, largely because I had never given myself over fully to the cause. I knew that even in my most devoted moments, I always held a part of myself back. I had felt this subtle distance created by my withholding for years, but only in leaving was I able to see that it wasn't because anyone was excluding me from the kind of connection I desired. I was unwilling to go to a certain level of commitment, a level of control that I was unwilling to surrender. I was left with the feeling at the end that I had failed to give enough of myself to either the company or to my family. My experience had been that both sides were always wanting more from me.

I began to see that this was no accident. Setting it up so people would be clamoring after me was how I reassured myself that I was wanted and valued, a strategy I had used since childhood when I discovered that the way to protect against being rejected or ignored was to become indispensable. To have others wanting more from you, even fighting over you, was a sure sign that you were not in danger of being disregarded and ensured that you were in a position to set your own terms.

In this situation, as in so many others in my life, I had succeeded in doing things my way and was careful not to give up too much of myself. This reflected the two primary concerns of my life: securing a place for myself where I experienced a sense of purpose and connectedness and maintaining the protection and control over my personal space, my separateness.

These longings were expressions of two deep fears; the first was a fear of being left alone without love or support, and the second was the fear of being swallowed up by the needs of others and losing myself. To keep my balance between these fears, I learned a dance to keep me from getting too close to either side.

My position at the company provided an ideal arena for me to play this out. Becoming too much of an insider would have prevented me from retaining the flexibility that I needed to adjust my ever-changing equilibrium. In addition, in doing things according to my desires, I saw to it I had no chance of losing myself, of being swallowed up by the system. I had gotten exactly what I had bargained for, although my lack of commitment had cost me, among other things, the sense of belonging I also sought.

Likewise with Linda and the kids, it wasn't simply a matter of being physically separated from them. I held myself at a distance by being distracted or preoccupied when I was with them. Though I could be and usually was fully present in the training room and had no trouble giving my complete attention to the students during the five days of the training, giving it at home on a long-term basis was another matter. My fear about losing myself to the needs of others made me gun-shy about the dangers of commitments and too many requirements on me.

The other side of this conflict was my desire to be close and to feel needed by people, which made the whole notion of marriage and family so appealing. Unfortunately, even at forty years of age, and with three children, I was still too emotionally immature to address all my needs and concerns. It continued to be a zero-sum game to me: relationships were about give-and-take, and that meant winners and losers. What was up for grabs was time, power, affection, support, and love.

My work at the company had been to teach people to operate with greater effectiveness in their lives, that is, to coach them toward behavior patterns that would enable them to become more competent at fulfilling their desires and needs. At guest events, I had promised them they would be able to get more of what they wanted in their lives from doing the training. What I was only now beginning to see was the cost of living life with a perpetual focus on fulfillment and personal gratification.

It was time to move beyond the dogma of the company and my identification as a trainer. What I was leaving was much more than a position or even a career. It was an attachment to a sense of myself as a separate entity whose overriding concern had to do with fulfilling his own egocentric interests, as opposed to a social being whose needs were inextricably interwoven with those of others.

I was starting to relate to the world from the context of relationships. Being born in this new way of being required a dying of the old way. The theory made sense. Unfortunately, or perhaps fortunately, I was unaware of what the rebirth process would entail.

Chapter 15

TRADING ROLES

Linda

Because Charlie had missed so much time with the children, we decided that he would be primary parent for a year and I would be the primary breadwinner. Finally, my frustrated desire to work could manifest after the five-year delay. Now that Sarah, our youngest, was starting school, I decided that I would let the ambitious professional woman within me step out.

The couples' workshop exceeded my expectations, but I soon learned that workshop delivery and design are the easy parts. Running a business is the huge task, requiring talent, skills, staff, and cooperation that we were determined to cultivate. The great success of the course validated my belief that we could produce our own workshops without the support of an outside organization. Buoyed by the course being a smash hit, I took the lead in building our budding business.

It was an exhilarating time for me. I was overjoyed by Charlie's recommitment to family and his change to become a sensitive, involved, nurturing father. Charlie had been working since he was fourteen years old, and the idea of being out of work for a time delighted him. He declared enthusiastically that in the extra time he would have, he would play his guitar, play tennis every day, and train for a marathon. I was skeptical about where he would find this time because I, myself, had been hard-pressed to get to Jazzercise on a regular basis with all I had to do each day. But I didn't say a word.

He had no concept of what running a household with three children entailed: the continuous tasks of shopping, cooking, laundry, dishes, and running the children to dance lessons, soccer practice, baseball practice, bowling, play dates, and Sunday school. He would find out on his own soon enough.

I was terrified about the challenge I was taking on, but I knew I wanted to do it. The sudden terror would strike my mind, making me think, "I don't know how to do this. I don't know how to be the breadwinner of this family. I can't do this; I'm going to fail." Then I would remind myself, "You didn't think you could keep the family together during those years that Charlie was on the road, and you did it. Creating a business is easier than that. He came back; he's with you now. You have his support. You can do this."

It was a chaotic period. We operated our new business, which we named the Empowerment Network, out of our home. With no spare bedroom to use as an office, we arranged two desks and a phone under a sunny window in our master bedroom. We had our best business planning meetings, visioning, and brainstorming nude in the bed. It was a scary time, being so close to the edge financially month after month and barely managing to pay our bills, and some months we didn't have enough money to pay them. But it was an exciting, creative time, and we were doing it together; that made all the difference. Sometimes it was glorious, and sometimes it was difficult.

The residual anger I still felt over Charlie's making work a priority over family quickly melted as I began to feel the burden of responsibility that men carry for financially supporting a family. It wasn't the long hours, although they were very long. It was the psychic weight of making it all work that I had never known before, and I don't think I could have understood Charlie's experience without living it. Charlie's profound appreciation for the work of being a full-time parent of three children was deeply gratifying to me. We were both moved by the newfound awareness that enabled us to appreciate each other to a much greater degree than we had in the past.

When our life calmed down, I began to understand why the whole, long ordeal had been so painful. I hadn't wanted to strike out on my own. I loved the idea of doing everything with Charlie. I didn't know that I was stunting my growth. Individuation, becoming who we are truly meant to be, cannot be accomplished without spending time alone.

Like many women, I had feared that my inner strength and ambition would be a threat to men. Furthermore, I feared that if I acted according to my ambition, I would neglect my children, and the family would suffer. This belief kept me from identifying my true nature. I had felt unfulfilled and looked for someone to blame. Envy of Charlie's professional success had fueled my resentment. I had been in a rage that he "kept" me from establishing my career. As I learned to know and love the ambitious part of me that I had judged as unacceptable, I allowed it freer expression and found it an ally, not an enemy. I observed my resentment toward Charlie disappearing.

Knowing that Charlie's position, as contract trainer was temporary, I felt an urgency to acquire the attributes that would allow me to make a success of our new business. Having been a traditional woman for most of my life, I found myself scrambling to learn assertiveness skills, to take the initiative, and to develop an action-and-results orientation. The challenge was demanding, confusing, and exhilarating. I learned that part of my motivation in denying my power had to do with my fear of being judged as unfeminine.

Recognizing the work that I needed to do to become an accomplished business manager, I sought to become more independent, looking for opportunities to strengthen myself as a person distinct from Charlie rather than continuing to see us as an inseparable team. In so doing, I came face-to-face with fear of being perceived as controlling, bitchy, and power hungry.

Rather than continue to try to conceal evidence of what could be perceived as unattractive qualities, I accepted the truth that I possessed some of these personality aspects and that they were not necessarily flaws. This recognition led to greater self-acceptance and to a strengthening of qualities necessary for effective entrepreneurship. The temptation to retreat to my past role as a supporter never completely disappeared, but I consistently chose not to yield to it.

Part of me didn't want to take this journey, but when I was forced to, I felt the pull back into the shelter of family and community. I wanted the daily protection of Charlie's big, strong, manly arms. I felt fragile and vulnerable out there alone. As I found greater awareness, I saw that the confusion that I had attributed to the relationship was actually due to my own inner struggle.

Charlie and I consciously and deliberately broke the distance-pursuer pattern that had characterized our relationship for so long. When there was no longer a struggle between Charlie and me, I had to face myself. I saw then the inner conflict between my desire to be an earth mother and an ambitious professional woman. The ambitious one, who had been stuffed down into the dark recesses of my shadow self, was banging on the trap door to get out.

When Charlie's six-month contract came to an end, my biggest concern was replacing the lost income with inflows from our fledgling business. I was concerned but not overly worried because I knew we could handle any challenge as long as we continued to work as partners.

I reestablished my counseling practice, and it began to grow. Our Partners in Commitment course was doing well. We had faith that if we continued to serve, we would have enough money to keep the family afloat. It was a tremendously exciting time because friends in other cities who wanted to take the course themselves put together classes for us. The vision I had of the two of us jetting around the country teaching together manifested again, only this time was more wonderful because we were on our own. We were finally free from the clutches of the company. I was energized and enthusiastic, like a racehorse let out of the starting gate. Charlie looked to me for some direction about how to organize our new business, and I was slightly shocked and very happy to find that I had an abundance of workable ideas. We started to be real collaborators.

Together we learned about sharing power. It was so clear to me how my well-being as an individual and our well-being as a couple was damaged during those corporate years because power was not shared jointly. During that five-year period, the script that Charlie held for the family was the one that prevailed—at my expense. We saw firsthand how not sharing power in a relationship is enormously detrimental. As soon as he resigned and did not have the corporation's agenda dictating so much of how we lived, we could move into the co-creative stage of our relationship, where we constantly collaborated about how we would design our lives. We finally became equals in decision making. Out of that collaboration and sharing of power, our relationship shot up on the happiness scale.

His old persona as "the knowing one" reared up at times, but most of the time I felt a blossoming of openness and trust in Charlie's word and intentions that I hadn't experienced for several years. The old feeling of being a betrayed victim was replaced by a strong sense of hopefulness and possibility. Self-pity and resentment were replaced by gratitude and self-confidence.

We were growing past that old hierarchical structure that had deadened our relationship. We were rebuilding the damaged trust through long, enjoyable conversations and sharing of our ideas. We each took responsibility for the part we had played in the breakdowns that had led to so much pain. We were immersed in the new theme of our relationship and the new theme of our relationships course, being each other's teacher and each other's student. We were determined to walk our talk. We came to understand that by holding each other as a teacher, learning to become flexible, and moving between the role of teacher and student, we became more whole.

Working together was not all a walk in the park, however. It involved serious stresses and strains. There were major adjustments to be made. I was frequently upset at what I perceived as Charlie's tendency to dominate and control, despite our agreement to work cooperatively in the room. He still had a way to go to shed the persona that he had developed over the years with the company. Sometimes he would take over in the workshop, and I frequently couldn't find a place to get a word in, which was a huge challenge because he was so sure that what he had to say was more important than what I had to say.

He was so much more experienced. I was in the position of apprentice to him and often held back, colluding in the view that his contributions were more important than my own. I accused him of stealing the spotlight and excluding me. It took months of having the same argument over and over before we worked out a policy whereby I would assert myself and step into the spotlight and Charlie would remember to step back and make space for me to speak to the group.

Meanwhile, back with the family, Charlie was discovering the extent of the damage from his absences. My efforts to have him understand how unhappy all three children were had fallen on deaf ears until he was home after resigning. At first, he was shocked to see just how out of control things were. The terrible truth that I had been facing for years—that we were no longer a healthy, loving family—struck him with sudden and considerable force.

At the same time, I was glad that he was finally up to seeing the truth of our difficult circumstances. At long last, my words were not falling on deaf ears. He knew firsthand that the children were cranky, irritable, and uncooperative at home and at school. I was tremendously encouraged by our now being a working team, spending hours assessing the damage and creating a design to rebuild the strength of the family. I was moving out of the role I had been cast in as an alarmist who was making too big a deal out of the children's lack of cooperation. We put together a plan for spending more time with the children, both as a group of five and with Charlie spending time with each child alone.

During the time that Charlie was the primary parent, he developed a beautiful closeness with all three children that he had never known before. His personality shifted in a major way during this period. He began to be more nurturing, gentle, patient, understanding, and generous. In essence, he was becoming a more sensitive and loving human being. But Charlie, still grieving his lost career, couldn't fully appreciate the flowering of his relationships in our family.

When Charlie's contract ended, we had a workshop schedule going well into the next year. Given the difference in our levels of skillfulness and experience, we went through many challenges in our seminars, some in full view of the students. We managed to use these incidents as grist for the mill of learning, both our own and our students. These experiences were painful and embarrassing but contributed to our growth. I had lots of energy. For the first time in years, I was expressing my gifts and talents, and beginning to own my power, I was confident and excited about possibilities. I was convinced that the worst was behind us.

Chapter 16

INTO THE ABYSS

Charlie

In February, around the time of my forty-first birthday, a feeling of unease began to greet me daily when I awoke. Critical, self-condemning thoughts bearing guilt and remorse followed, as did a pervasive sense of inadequacy. Despite my efforts to eject these uninvited guests, they refused to leave.

I found myself obsessively reviewing all the important decisions I'd ever made, particularly those within the last few years. In a few short weeks, what had begun as a series of doubts soon turned into assertions, then accusations, and finally condemnation. I was my own arresting officer, judge, jury, and torturer.

"Maybe we never should have moved to California. Maybe the damage done to the family while I was at the company is irreparable, and the kids will never be okay. Maybe we chose the wrong town to live in. Maybe I'm nothing but a fraud. I'm too weak, selfish, lazy, stupid, unimaginative, and self-indulgent. I'm a terrible father and a worthless husband. I've made my wife miserable. I'm a hypocrite, and I have absolutely no integrity. It's too late to do anything about any of this. The damage is done. A person as degenerate and worthless as I am should never have become a parent in the first place."

These thoughts weren't opinions. To me, they were incontestable facts that I was finally recognizing now that I was no longer smoking the dope of my high-profile career. With each passing day, the quantity and intensity of this negative thinking increased, beating me down. I was consumed by an orgy of self-recrimination that I felt completely unable to overcome.

At first, I tried to keep this from Linda. I felt overwhelmed with shame and didn't want to burden her with additional problems to those that she already had. My efforts to conceal my distress proved futile, however. I was unaware of how transparent my distress was. When she informed me that it had become obvious to her that things were not going well with me, I felt both relieved and embarrassed. She said that she had noticed that I had recently become increasingly withdrawn, distant, impatient, and irritable. I acknowledged that I had been feeling a little blue, but I downplayed it, insisting that it was connected to leaving the company and that the feelings would soon pass. They didn't.

By the beginning of spring, I could no longer deny either to myself or to Linda that I was in the midst of a deep depression. I needed help, but despite the agonizing days and sleepless nights, I refused to see a therapist. I saw myself as competing in a contest and was determined to defeat my opponent. Depression was the enemy. To see a therapist would be an admission of failure, and it would confirm that something was wrong with me, as though by not getting help, I was proving that I was really okay. Considering that I had spent years as a therapist and family counselor supporting people, this thinking was ironic, even crazy.

But something else was going on besides me trying to macho my way through this. Twenty-five years earlier, when I witnessed the deterioration of my father's life as the result of a series of debilitating episodes of bipolar psychosis, I promised myself that I would not, under any conditions, accept this as my legacy. I feared that, like my father, my life was destined to be destroyed by uncontrollable internal forces. What I had believed for much of my life was that a time bomb was ticking away inside me and would one day explode in my brain like it had in his. When it did, my life would be forever, irreversibly destroyed and, like him, I would lose everything: my work, my family, my self-respect, my property, my friends, my happiness, my health, my sanity, and my control.

The bomb exploded in my father when I was seventeen and he was forty-seven. I was convinced that with sufficient strength, willpower, and determination I could prevent a collapse. It would require continual vigilance and relentless self-control, but I would do whatever it took. This commitment felt like a matter of life or death, and from the moment I made it, nothing else in my life mattered as much as keeping my promise to stay on top of things, to remain in control, and to do whatever needed to be done to keep it all together.

Unfortunately, I was completely unconscious of this commitment and the enormously destructive consequences of being possessed by it. Until the intensity of the depression cracked the wall of my willful determination, I hadn't seen the terror that had shaped most of the choices I had made for much of my life. After nearly twenty-five years of straining under the burden of compulsively trying to keep myself and my world under control, things were beginning to unravel. Despite my intensified, panic-stricken attempts to repair the ever-more-increasing number of breaks in the dike, I began sensing that my efforts were futile. The facade I had constructed over my shame and insecurity was crumbling. It seemed as if there was nothing I could do to prevent an inevitable collapse.

The main means that I had used in the past to alleviate my feelings of guilt, shame, unworthiness, and inadequacy that surfaced in me periodically was immersion in work. For me, and for many of the other trainers, work was the substance of choice for mood management. Of course, most of us imbibed alcohol and/or an assortment of other substances, but nothing could match the high of being in the training room. Even the most painful or unpleasant feelings would instantly dissolve in the presence of the energy, attention, and power that were available in the front of the room.

Self-doubts and feelings of insecurity instantly dissolved when I was in a room full of believers who were convinced of their leader's all-knowing wisdom and supernatural powers. I was, of course, one of the believers in the students' projections of omniscience onto me. Not only did I agree with them; I also insisted on being seen and treated accordingly. Now, with my primary means of distraction and self-medication no longer available, the undercurrent of negativity, like rust beneath a new coat of paint, began to seep corrosively through, at first in the form of barely noticeable feelings, then in despair. These feelings were compounded in proportion to the degree to which my self-perception and the students' perception of me had been distorted and inflated.

As a trainer, my authority would typically be tested in the course of a seminar. In the process of successfully meeting these challenges, my credibility and trustworthiness would be established as I demonstrated my competence. Much of what went into creating such "credibility" often involved coercion, intimidation, and other forms of manipulation. The students' willingness to trust this kind of authority is based on a deep desire to believe in the healing and redemptive powers of the leader.

As others see us, so we tend to see ourselves. The experience of being viewed and related to this way only reinforced my feelings of grandiosity. Part of the unspoken code of the company was not to overtly display the arrogance that generally went along with the position. The "crime" was not in believing in our omnipotence but in getting caught at it. The successful cultivation of the trainer image required the development of a façade of false humility.

A skilled facilitator could even make mistakes and have them reinforce his or her superior image. On many occasions, students expressed admiration that I had acknowledged having made a mistake. Everything becomes part of building the mystique of the trainer. For any of us to avoid being taken in by the charade was virtually impossible. We were all always smoking our own dope.

As with any addiction, the addict undergoes a period of withdrawal when the substance isn't available. Symptoms of withdrawal include irritability, heightened sensitivity to criticism, impatience, self-judgment, free-floating anxiety, depression, and fatigue. This was a function of having pulled the plug that propelled the steady flow of adrenaline and endorphins into the bloodstream, allowing me to remain in a nearly constant state of hyperstimulation. By comparison, "ordinary" life was desolate and boring. For this reason, any trainer spending more than a couple of weeks out of the training room was extremely rare. Although a common lament was how overworked and tired we were, the truth was that none of us would have had it any other way.

For the first six months after resigning, I had done remarkably well, considering that I was only spending five days a month in the room. That was supplemented by at least one couples' workshop that Linda and I taught. As Linda was still very much junior to me in experience and mostly in the background, I was able to hustle up a few more days a month of attention to feed my habit.

But by April, it was no longer working. Suddenly, my confidence was gone. I was deflated. The energy, power, and self-assurance that had carried me for the past several years were rapidly leaking out. No longer able to keep up the front with Linda, I fell into the pit of self-hate and despair. The demons were no longer at the door; they had broken it down and were inside the house tearing things up and roaring with glee at the misery and shame that was my due for selfishness and grandiosity.

Eventually, I lost the ability to experience pleasure of any kind. I had no appetite for food, sex, or anything else. I developed insomnia, rarely sleeping more than three hours a night. I lost my ability to concentrate or think about anything other than my own self-hatred and the anxiety I felt regarding, what looked to me to be, an impossibly dismal future. I felt enormous guilt over the damage that I had caused to others. I couldn't look at the children or even think of them without feeling overcome with sorrow.

I was flooded with nonstop self-loathing that usually peaked in the hours between midnight and dawn. I often woke Linda to listen to my obsessive ruminating because it was one of the only ways that I could find peace. These interruptions to her sleep eventually left Linda exhausted until she finally put her foot down and insisted that I allow her to get the rest she needed, lest we both go down the drain together. In addition to handling all the business and family responsibilities on her own, Linda now had what amounted to another full-time job: caring for someone who required increasing amounts of time, attention, reassurance, and comfort.

In May, Linda insisted that I see a psychiatrist who had been recommended by a friend. She was adamant, and I had neither the strength nor the will to resist. Weakly protesting to the end I told myself that I was less of a failure because she had taken the initiative. After all, it wasn't *my* idea.

Linda drove me to San Francisco for the appointment. I jabbered obsessively throughout the forty-five-minute drive. When we arrived at his office, a tall, bearded, distinguished-looking man who looked to be in his mid-sixties came into the waiting room to greet us and showed both Linda and me into his treatment room. Jack was a traditionally trained psychiatrist who combined conventional psychoanalytic treatment with various forms of alternative healing.

"You're not manic-depressive," he pronounced after listening to a synopsis of my situation, reassuring me that my worst fear was ungrounded. Then came the *but*. "But you're going through a process of inner healing that is going to take a while, and things will probably get worse before they get better—a lot worse."

He then summarized my situation: "For the past six years, you've been a con man, using your power to hustle unsuspecting people who trust you. You used them for your own self-centered purposes, to feed your massively insecure ego, to keep the chairs in the training room filled to make your boss happy so that you can gain his approval. You've totally neglected and abused your wife and children, and they've been damaged in the process. Your oldest son is probably going to put you through more hell than you can imagine. What you are currently experiencing is the guilt that is healthy and appropriate given the nature of your past deeds.

"Your problem is that you don't like it and you want to be relieved of it. You want some pill to take it away from you because it hurts too much. Well, I hate to sound callous, but to put it bluntly, you've got it coming to you. As you yourself have probably said to others, 'you created this reality,' and you've got to deal with it, which in this case means opening up to let yourself feel the full measure of the consequences of what you've done. After you've done that—and there's no telling how long that process might take—then you and I can do the real work, the hard work of finding out just how it was that you got yourself into such a mess. Then we'll see what in your life experience made your desire for power so strong that you were willing to sell yourself and your family out in order to get it."

Clearly, Jack did not subscribe to the hand-holding school of supportive psychiatry, not that I would have preferred that style. I appreciated and respected something about his no-bullshit approach. Still, it wasn't easy to hear.

"If you decide to work with me," he continued, going on without waiting for a response, "we're going to have to get a few things straight. First of all, you should understand that I've worked with a lot people like you, who have experienced what you're going through. I won't negotiate treatment because I know more about this than you do. I'll be making recommendations that I will expect you to follow. If you don't like what I'm saying or suggesting, go find someone that you can con and manipulate."

I told Jack that I wanted to work with him and thanked him for his frankness. I asked if he had any suggestions that might help me sleep better or diminish some of the other physical and emotional symptoms that I was experiencing. He prescribed an antidepressant medication, warning me that it might take a few weeks for it to take effect and that, even then, it might not work. He told me that there were no instant cures for depression and that I had better learn to deal with these feelings until one way or another they were gone.

Leaving Jack's office with a prescription and an appointment for the following week, I felt hopeful for the first time in months, clinging to Jack's words that the feelings would go away. On the drive back, I said to Linda, "I think that we've broken the cycle. I feel like there's some light at the end of the tunnel and it might not be long before this is all behind us." Though Linda didn't protest, to me, she obviously didn't share my newfound optimism. "That's okay," I thought. "We're on the upswing, and pretty soon she'll see that as clearly as I do."

Once again, Linda's cautiousness proved to be a more accurate assessment of my state than my unbridled optimism. Twenty-four hours after my appointment with Jack, I was deep in despair again. I looked forward to my next appointment like a starving man looks forward to a meal. I had pinned all my hopes of salvation on him.

A week later at my second appointment, Jack asked me to tell him about my family life when I was growing up. I wanted to discuss specific ways of alleviating my symptoms, and I was impatient to get on with things. I didn't want to rehash old news. Jack reminded me that if we were going to work together, I was going to have to accept his direction even though my inflated ego hated not having control.

At the end of the ninety minutes, we set up our next weekly appointment. "How long do you think this is going to take," I asked, failing miserably in my attempt to conceal my impatience.

"Longer than you want it to," Jack answered. "You're going to have to learn that the world doesn't run according to your timetable, that you have to accept things that your ego doesn't like. The more you struggle, the harder it's going to be. Any other questions?"

I left feeling both angry and relieved that I couldn't bullshit Jack, and I was grateful that he had the toughness and understanding I knew I would need to get through this. I looked forward to my weekly meetings with him, not just because I felt he was my last hope but also because the appointments provided my life with some structure. My days were otherwise without direction or focus, and I had little motivation to do anything. The hours dragged, as I spent my days sitting on the couch or lying in bed consumed by negative thoughts. I could do nothing to free myself from their grip, and the more consumed by them I became, the more immobilized I felt.

I was embarrassed by my nonproductivity, but I didn't feel as though I could do anything about it. I felt depleted, and I kept expecting Linda to finally get fed up with me and threaten me with an ultimatum or simply refuse to continue caring for me. I was convinced that she was viewing me through eyes that mirrored my own intolerance. It seemed inconceivable to me that she could continue caretaking this vegetable in a man's body. I checked with her constantly to see how close she was to giving up on me. I lived in terror of losing her, of driving her away with my neediness. Every time she reassured me, I felt like a prisoner who had been given a stay of execution. Linda's presence provided a soothing balm that softened the painful thoughts and feelings that were consuming me, but the respite was only temporary. Within hours or even minutes, the raging pain would be back, as though I hadn't heard a word she said.

In the meantime, there were the kids. Eben and Sarah, at ten and eight, respectively, were too young to understand, but Jesse, at fourteen, was more aware of my disintegration. Lost and overwhelmed in a new school to which he had recently transferred, because we could no longer afford to keep any of the kids in private school, he acted out his feelings in the form of aggressive, irresponsible, and disrespectful behavior. We received frequent messages from the school and sometimes visits from the police informing us that Jesse had found yet another creative way of expressing his pain. When he wasn't getting himself into trouble outside the house, he was often making everyone's life at home a living hell.

Besides the loneliness and confusion that he was experiencing at school, Jesse was angry with me for having abandoned him for the past several years. He chose ways of expressing himself that were designed not only to send a clear message home to Linda and me but also to hurt us in a way that our neglect had hurt him. By becoming a known troublemaker in the small town in which we lived and creating the reputation of being destructive and hostile in school and on the streets, Jesse damaged both Linda's and my professional reputations.

Where Jesse needed the support of consistent, loving limits, all I could give him was anger when he failed to respond to my impotent requests for his cooperation. We were locked in a battle of wills in which I continually found myself defeated. Neither my voice nor my actions reflected authority. My response to Jesse's refusal to take my threats seriously was to become still more frustrated with myself. His defiance served to validate my own powerlessness, leaving me feeling humiliated. Meanwhile, Jesse kept prodding me to get a response that would reassure him he was not the most powerful male in the family, a position he outwardly wanted but inwardly didn't. He was willing to get physical in his efforts to test the waters.

I desperately craved some sense of potency. The pain I felt in watching Linda struggle to keep everything together while Jesse tyrannized the family was excruciating. I felt like I was tied up and watching everyone being assaulted—except that I was simultaneously the guilty assailant as well as the helpless onlooker. It was my own weakness that had created this horror, and I hated it with every fiber of my being.

What I didn't understand at the time was that my ongoing self-contempt and my attachment to guilt were perpetuating the show. It would only be much later that I would be able to understand that the cycle would be broken only by compassion and self-forgiveness. These were the very things that I felt unworthy to receive from myself or anyone else.

In the meantime, Jesse had a decidedly different way of dealing with his self-image issues. Rather than internalizing his pain, he externalized it by turning our home into a war zone. The more frightened he felt, the more aggressive he became. The more aggressive he became, the harder I tried to control him. Too confused and overwhelmed myself to think clearly and offer the guidance and structure that Jesse needed, I became a reaction machine, responding to his outbursts with threats and attempts to physically restrain him. As anyone who has ever dealt with an adolescent in a similar situation knows, this type of reactivity is the interpersonal equivalent of pouring gasoline on a fire. And at times, our home felt very much like an inferno.

Jesse seemed determined to make a mockery of my "authority," which, given my condition, was hardly much of a challenge. I would send him to his room, and he would refuse to go. I would drag him there, and he would run out. I would bar the door, and he would go out the window and climb down to the ground. We yelled at each other. We fought. He smashed plates and chairs, kicked in doors, and punched holes in walls. In one of our fights, he pulled a long hunting knife on me. I wrestled it out of his hands, barely. Then I just sat down and cried. I cried for Jesse; I cried for myself; I cried for all of us. There was nothing but pain in this miserable life, and I saw no possibility of there ever being anything else. I wanted to die, but I couldn't consider suicide because of what I knew that would do to the rest of the family.

After three months of therapy, I questioned the point of continuing a process that was costing over seven hundred dollars a month when we had little in the way of income and nothing in reserve. Our health insurance did not cover outpatient psycho-therapy. I was having trouble justifying the expense. Although I was sleeping better thanks to Xanax, I wasn't feeling like therapy was going anywhere.

In my final session with Jack, I told him that I had decided to stop therapy. My reason was that we couldn't afford it and that my constant worry about the money was just adding to my problems. Maybe, I reasoned weakly, if I could stop the flow of money pouring out of the family so much faster than it was coming in, I might be able to get a better grip on things. Jack softened his characteristically challenging style, saying, "I understand that you feel it's better to stop now. That's okay. But I want you to understand that what you're going through is bigger than anything you can handle on your own. Don't be ashamed to get help when you need it."

Chapter 17

CHARLIE'S DEPRESSION

Linda

After years of feeling insignificant and weak, I was ready to accept a huge challenge, and I felt confident to meet it. Charlie's descent into depression left me feeling grateful that I was strong enough to be able to support him. Hearing his fears was scary, but I had complete confidence that we would come through this dark time. One day he turned to me. "Are you willing to go into the pits of hell with me?" I answered, "Of course, I will go anywhere with you." He then led me down into the dark pit, where all his demons of remorse, regret, mistakes, failures, inadequacies, guilt, shame, fear, neediness, and even death lived.

I had accompanied many clients over the years into the dark, secret recesses of their minds, but I had never gone this deep nor stayed so long. All my skill and experience as a therapist, coupled with my love for Charlie, enabled me now to accompany him. There were times when Charlie's depression was so severe that he didn't want to go on living. During these times, our bond and his trust in me were strong enough that he would listen to me. If ever I were in a position to exploit his vulnerability, it was now. But I didn't.

We journeyed in the bed, naked, pressed tightly together, skin to skin, wrapped in each other's arms and legs. A bit like a sexual experience, allowing my boundaries to become permeable, I was able to merge with him and, in the blending of our energies, to face his demons. Close enough to breathe each other's breath, he reported what he was feeling, and I felt his fear in my body. Plagued with guilt for having abused the power of his position as a trainer to manipulate people with strong-arm tactics, fear, and intimidation, he kept saying, "I hurt so many people. I hurt so many people." I answered him with "I know you have done harm, but your strength will come back, and you can make amends. There is time for you to balance the harm with acts of loving kindness." His trembling vibrated in me. His heart pounded inside me. When he sobbed his sorrow over his regrets, mistakes, and failure, I sobbed with him.

Charlie cried out, "I've done everything wrong. I've made such a mess. My career is over. I'm going to lose everything. I've ruined the children. Things are never going to get better." I held him and felt his despair, knowing at the same time that his perspective was distorted. I knew we could repair the damage to the children. I didn't deny its extent, but there was time. "We have Jesse for four more years before he leaves home," I said. "And with the younger children, we have even more time. We have enough love to undo the damage. We're together now; we're a team. We'll do it. You're just exhausted from overwork. You're grief-stricken discovering all the things you haven't been able to see when you were going so fast."

I thought perhaps it was karmic justice for all the years Charlie had denied his dependency. I teased him that this was his just reward for pretending to be so autonomous and hyper-independent. Charlie couldn't believe that I could still love him when he couldn't work or support the family. To him that he could be loved just for himself, not for what he produced, was incomprehensible. But that was the case. I loved him more for being real. From my own experience, I knew that the success I was experiencing had resulted from my own dark night of the soul. I told Charlie, "Your career is far from over. You will be an incredible healer with deep compassion and understanding from having visited the pits of hell." And as I said these reassuring things about the children's recovery, his recovery, his career blossoming, I was absolutely certain that it was all true.

Although very close, I was not completely absorbed into his experience. I kept a piece of my own frame of reference. When Charlie felt that he was drowning in the whirlpool of his despair, my conviction that his suffering was not pointless offered a steady counterpull out of the swirl. I knew there was meaning in going through these horrors.

"There is no need to fear being trapped here," I told him. "I can see a bit of daylight. There is a way out. Just stay near me, I will lead you up to the light this time, and I will help so you can come out of the darkness permanently." I kept holding my conviction out for him to lean on. I held him in my arms while he cried. I held him while he shook with fear. I kept repeating what an incredible healer he would be after this hideous journey to the underworld and how many more people he could guide.

What I could see that Charlie couldn't was that he had asked for the teachings he needed to prepare him for his next work. He hadn't bargained for the lessons coming in the form of a suicidal depression. I kept reminding him that he was being prepared to do deep and holy work, that he was facing all his demons so he could help others face theirs. I spoke with complete authority and conviction.

I had been to my own darkness. I had faced my biggest demon—loneliness—during all those years of days and nights by myself. Now I was on the other side, enjoying an ongoing sense of connection to others and myself. The mourning that I experienced when I felt like an "abandoned orphan" and "the grieving widow" began to subside when I let myself experience the pain. My loneliness had not been in vain. I had gotten to know deeper parts of myself. I had learned how resourceful, powerful, and independent I could be on my own. How else could I have found out unless I lived it?

I felt certain that, with our relationship healing so quickly, our love and alignment could set a new tone in the family that would heal the deprivation. I said over and over, and he finally picked up the chant, "We have time to undo the damage. Together we'll create a loving family."

Charlie was facing his greatest fear, his fear of going crazy and, being unproductive, losing everything including my love. When he shook all over, his judging mind railed at him: "You weak coward." And my response was, "Oh no; on the contrary, you have the courage of a warrior to face your greatest fear." He needed to hear me say over and over that his pain wasn't senseless but had a purpose. It was easy for me to reassure him. I just kept drawing on my own experience. I spoke of how I had lived in terror of infidelity. In my family, the affairs and the secrecy around them had poisoned the trust in my parents' marriage. I could not stave off that demon of fear that wanted to swallow me: that Charlie would go away, bed down with someone else, and not return. Through his repeated departures, resisting so many opportunities to indulge in sexual escapades, and always choosing to come home to me, the wild demons of jealousy and fear finally shut up.

I knew that all our unskillful fighting had meaning too. We had learned what a toll it takes—the searing of the tender flesh of the relationship. It was the suffering from the fighting that awakened in us a commitment to living a life of nonharm, to learn to deal with our differences with goodwill, generosity, spaciousness, self-discipline, and respect. The pain of every single harsh word we had used became the compost that fertilized our relationship and turned it into a lush garden.

Charlie kept encountering an image of death that called to him with promises of relief from the pain. Stubbornly refusing medication, he spent months facing off with death. He repeatedly chose to bear the pain, dragging himself through one more day to perform small acts of kindness to make up for some of the harm he felt he had caused others. Each day, he would come up with some kind, loving thing he could do for me, the children, or someone else.

He had so little energy that getting out of bed to make breakfast for the children and pack their lunches was a big accomplishment. After he got them off to school, he would have to go back to bed. He struggled to keep functioning at a minimal level and would not be seduced by death's promise of an easy out. Very gradually, Charlie began to see that being dependent on me didn't mean I would take control, put a ring through his nose, lead him around on a leash, and have him do my bidding as if he were a slave. He needed to know down to his toes that when he was helpless and out of control; I wouldn't exploit his vulnerability.

He was questioning everything, filled with self-doubt. "You don't respect me anymore, do you?" he would say, more a statement of fact than a question. "You think I'm weak." I responded, "On the contrary, my heart is filled with compassionate understanding and great respect for your willingness to stand in the fire of your pain." I knew this wasn't a permanent condition. I repeated my heartfelt assurances that Charlie was learning what he needed to understand dependence, inter-dependence, and what it means to be a nurturing, involved parent.

Now, suddenly, I had elevated status. He called me his lifeline. He told me I was the only thing between him and death. He kept thanking me for keeping him alive. Only months before, I had been accused of being a ball and chain, of being an anchor weighing him down, of preventing him from soaring to the heights he wanted to fly to. Now I was some kind of savior. Only months before, his idea of himself in relation to me had been that he was too good for me. Now he kept telling me I was too good for him, that he didn't deserve my love and commitment. I didn't want to be a savior any more than I wanted to be a ball and chain. I just wanted to be regular people with ordinary problems and not live in such drama.

For me, after so many years of seeing myself and being seen as the weak one of the pair, having a chance to be the strong one was wonderful. It was music to my ears to hear Charlie's apology, "I can't believe how long I believed I was too good for you." After so many years of drought, of not hearing much acknowledgment and, to a large extent, being taken for granted, I was like a parched field of dried grass getting regular drenchings. The rain soothed my dryness and then nourished me until I was lush with tall grass and wildflowers.

After Charlie resigned from the company, I went to a furniture store and bought a beautiful king-sized bed. The kids liked to pile into bed with us on weekend mornings when we had time to hang out together. They were getting bigger now, and we needed more space to fit all five of us. The bed was a symbol of the family togetherness for which I had been longing for years. And we did use it for that, but little did I know when I bought it that I would be spending so much time in that bed, holding Charlie because he was too exhausted and depressed to get out of it. Our life narrowed to the bed and had a certain flavor of our first infatuation stage, only this time we weren't sharing the slim single bed we shared in the sixties.

When Charlie finally left the company, after his consulting contract wasn't renewed, he received no acknowledgment of the years of devoted service, no thank-you for the many personal sacrifices he and his family had made on behalf of the courses and the company. I had observed this coldness on departure before with friends who had left. As soon as you are no longer part of the organization, you cleared your personal belongings from your desk, and they sent your final check in the mail. There is no party, no gift, no testimonials about your years of contribution—nothing. You just go home. No one ever called. Although he never complained about it, I knew that he was deeply wounded after having given everything he had—his time, energy, and creativity. I was appalled. It became clear that he would never have anything to do with the company again.

His depression began gradually but deepened before my eyes. He stopped doing his workouts. When he stopped reading, I got scared because he had always been such a voracious reader, reading magazines or the newspaper while waiting to turn the pancakes over and always having a half-dozen books out of the library at any given time and reading pieces of each every day.

After years of looking forward to the time when Charlie would leave the company and come back into the family, here it was. I was so happy when he announced he was leaving, I laughed and cried at the same time. But the expectation that things would straighten out as soon as he left his demanding job was not met. We now had new challenges. When I think back to the year that was the absolute worst of his life, it's disturbing to me that it was one of my best.

In addition to the exhilaration I felt in my professional expansion, I was thrilled to have Charlie home. In his incapacitation, he was prevented from engaging in his normal activity; he had to just be. He took time to talk to me, to really see me, to appreciate me. I was no longer the old shoe he took for granted; now I felt like a precious jewel. The intimacy I had been yearning for with my whole being had at last arrived! We spent hours talking, touching, and making love. Charlie looked into my eyes when we spoke. It had always been a bone of contention between us that when we talked in bed, he lay on his back and spoke to the ceiling while I lay on my side looking at him but unable to make eye contact. Now, as he looked to me to find the comfort that was unavailable within him, I was finally experiencing the eye-to-eye connection I had hungered for. For the first time in my life, I had my fill of intimacy.

He told me he was feeling so much love for me and was frustrated at not being strong enough to show his love by being a better provider. This desire to do something to make me happy got poured into our lovemaking. We took extended periods, with exquisite mindfulness to every caress. I finally got to live out my favorite fantasy of being the revered queen. My brain must have been pouring endorphins into my bloodstream from the extended erotic stimulation. I walked around in a euphoric state.

He didn't leave the house very often. In the grand scheme of things, it seemed like a necessary healing for our family. He was home when the children returned from school, he was there at dinner, and he was there to read them stories at bedtime. Our life had a simplicity that we hadn't known for years. Charlie's life was stripped down to the essentials. And, after being deprived of him for so long, that simple contact was exactly what the children needed. During that year, he truly reconnected with them. The depth of his connection with the children enabled me to step back from the mommy role.

Charlie's normal way of being is associated with the archetype of Hermes, the god with winged feet. His usual pace of life is fast moving. When he was depressed, with so little energy, he had to slow down. I was delighted by no longer having to chase him. My pace tends to be a lot slower. We were more closely matched at that time and spent hours just being together in the way I liked, talking quietly, gazing into each other's eyes. How genuine, real, and raw he was at that time was compelling, and I delighted in being sought after. I had always been the pursuer and Charlie the distancer. To be pursued was wonderful!

During this time, Charlie was getting some of the lessons he needed to become a good lover. He was learning about receiving, about letting me in to see his vulnerability, and about intimacy. I was learning about individuation, going out into the world to make my way. Though I was doing a tremendous amount of giving, I had no resentment. My giving flowed freely from a pure well. The care giving that I had done while Charlie worked for the company was steeped in resentment. I've never wanted to give on demand. I wanted to give when I wanted to give; I wanted it to be my choice.

Now that I was feeling such compassion for Charlie's suffering, the voice in my mind was saying, "He's contrite. He's apologized for hurting me. He's so sincere and genuine." His humility activated my protective, nurturing instincts. I only wanted to support him to heal and move through this crisis. I didn't believe that the depression was anything more than fleeting, a price that would have to be paid for Charlie's living too high and too fast for too long.

When after several months, his depression showed no signs of lifting I became seriously worried about him. I began, at first tentatively, to express my opinion that he should see a doctor for antidepressant medication. But each time I brought the subject up, Charlie adamantly refused. Even though my confidence and strength had grown, I was still in recovery from the long struggle to keep the family together. At the time I didn't have the clarity or certainty to say, "Charlie, you are out of it. You're lost. You need medical attention and medication. Just get in the car; I'm taking you to the doctor."

I was still partially possessed by the old habit of elevating Charlie and deferring to his judgment. I continued to allow his will to prevail. As the weeks went by, I grew more alarmed over his deterioration. His suffering finally reached the point where my not insisting on his getting help was impossible. It was starting to feel like a matter of life or death. A trusted friend gave me the name of a psychiatrist in San Francisco who had worked extensively with people, mostly men, who had experienced the kind of letdown and remorse Charlie was going through. Jack nailed the situation immediately, but his treatment didn't do much to alleviate Charlie's depression. He wanted Charlie to commit to long-term therapy and address issues relating to his family of origin. Charlie needed something more immediate. He did put him on an antidepressant, and we prayed it would work. It didn't.

Chapter 18

Way Too Much Drama

Linda

I continued organizing couples' courses around the country and bring Charlie with me to co-facilitate them. Miraculously, he was still able to step into his professional persona and the students didn't seem to realize that anything was amiss. During a weekend course on Cape Cod, his other self came into the room. As soon as I put the students in an exercise and there were a few minutes to spare, he began spilling out all his depressive thoughts. I was supporting him on breaks, running the course, and listening to him while the students wrote in their notebooks after doing an exercise. I sat there hoping that the students near us couldn't hear what he was saying. Meanwhile, Charlie seemed oblivious to everyone and everything around him.

During the lunch break of the second day, Charlie and I walked on the beach. He told me that he couldn't go on this way. Life was just too painful. Once again he spoke of suicide. I tried to help him as best I could, and we went back to the training room to complete the rest of the course. It was hot in the room, and I suddenly began to feel claustrophobic, like I was going to jump out of my skin.

The last exercise of the day was for the group to write love poems. We had all the students regroup outside under some big shade trees. While they were writing, Charlie leaned over to me and out of his gloom and pessimism said, "No one is going to read their poem." This is every seminar leader's worst nightmare: you open up sharing with the group, and not one single person is willing to share.

Fortunately, many people read beautiful, elegant love poems. By this point I was so exhausted and depleted that I couldn't speak. Charlie finished the course, and the evaluation forms came back as strong as ever. I felt certain that guardian angels were watching over us.

Our next course was scheduled for Little Rock, Arkansas. We left the house in the morning to catch our flight; I drove, and Charlie sat silently amid the blackness that had become his recurrent mood. We arrived at the airport, checked in, and then got in line while our plane began boarding; suddenly as our flight was boarding, Charlie was hit with an immobilizing panic attack. He told me, "I can't go. I can't board the plane."

"What do you mean?" I asked, beginning to feel panic myself.

"I can't go on this trip with you. I'm sorry. I hate to let you down, and I know that you want me to go, but I can't. I just can't."

He explained that for years he had been endlessly getting on planes, abandoning the children, and he didn't want to leave them one more time. They needed him. Trying to steady myself, I reminded him how present he had been with the children in recent months, how they were starting to trust again.

His legs seemed to slowly collapse underneath him, and he slid down the wall he was leaning against and sat down on the floor near the gate. "Something terrible is going to happen to me if I go." Then he started to cry. Hearing him, people around and behind us stared, their attention first drawn because the line had stopped moving. His symptoms were full-blown: his heart was racing, and he was drenched with sweat. He could barely catch his breath, and his legs suddenly could no longer support him. Charlie told me later that this moment was the event he had dreaded for so long. He was thinking, "This is it: the complete meltdown. Either I'm dying or I'm losing my mind as well as control over my body.

The people watching us probably thought he was phobic about flying and having an anxiety attack. One of the other passengers came over and, kneeling in front of us, asked if he was all right. Charlie couldn't say anything; he just looked up at him. I thanked him but declined his assistance. Now people were stepping around us. Charlie was oblivious to the whole scene. He alternately cried and spoke a garbled monologue about guilt and shame and the punishment and suffering that he believed he deserved for causing so many people so much pain.

Once again, I brought myself into the horror that Charlie was experiencing and tried to literally join him in his world. I held him against me, took his hand, and turned my head toward him until our eyes were locked into each other's. "It's okay. You're going to be all right," I said softly but firmly. "This is just a bad time you're having. It's not the end, and it's not a permanent condition. It's just temporary, and soon it's going to be over, and you're going to be fine. You're not alone. I'm with you. We're going to make it. I promise."

Gradually, he began to calm down. His breathing slowed, and his eyes began to soften as if he was coming out of a trance. Once again, I was able to soothe him enough that he could pull out of his terror. I knew that he was listening to me; I was getting through to him. "We will call the children every day from Arkansas." I repeated again the healing mantra: "We have time to heal the family. It's going to be okay."

A couple of airline employees were standing a few feet away watching us with curiosity and concern. The line was gone; the door of the gate was still open. Silently, Charlie stood slowly. Together we walked onto the plane.

We landed in Little Rock three hours later. The workshop began the next morning at nine o'clock. As had been usual, I took the lead in facilitating the weekend. Despite Charlie remaining firmly planted in the background, he made some beautiful contributions to the course. There were some moments when I began to buckle under the pressure and started seeing things through Charlie's distorted perceptions. During our next course, he spent the breaks telling me how teenagers who isolate themselves from their parents don't reveal that they're suffering and end up committing suicide. I was suddenly convinced that was happening with our teenage son, Jesse. We made a panicky call home to make sure he was still alive. Again, ever the professionals, miraculously, the seminar went well.

Two weeks after our return from Little Rock I announced that we needed a family vacation. All those years that Charlie worked for the company we hardly ever went on a family vacation. I resolved that we would take the three kids to Washington, D.C., and then to New York City to visit my brother. We were going to do what happy families do. Charlie expressed his dread that our vacation might turn into a disaster but said he felt obligated to accommodate me. He was so weak that he was unable to effectively protest or resist anything I wanted. We made arrangements to combine business with a visit to Washington, D.C., and New York City.

We arrived on the East Coast in the middle of a blazing heat wave. It was in the nineties every day, and the humidity was very high. After facilitating a couples' workshop in Virginia, the five of us spent three days sightseeing. Washington was experiencing an unbearably hot and oppressively humid heat wave, and it seemed that every sane person had left the city. One afternoon, while walking across the Washington Mall on our way to the Smithsonian Museum, both Eben and Sarah complained that they were too hot and tired to go on. Rather than allowing them to rest, Charlie picked them both up, put them on each of his shoulders, and carried them to the museum. He refused to accommodate my insistence that he put them down, as if he derived a perverse, masochistic kind of pleasure in punishing himself to the point of exhaustion in the unbearable heat, as though such torture was in some way redemptive.

The next day we took a train to New York, where we stayed with my brother in Lower Manhattan. From there, our "vacation" went from bad to worse. Charlie had miscalculated his supply of the Xanax he had become so dependent on and had run out while we were in Washington. Experiencing the hyperanxiety that results from the sudden withdrawal from this very addictive drug, he contacted doctors, pharmacists, and friends on both coasts, trying unsuccessfully to get a refill. No luck. Charlie said that he felt like he literally wanted to jump out of his skin. He couldn't stop moving. Meanwhile, my morbid obsessions intensified.

After an exhausting day climbing the Statue of Liberty, we arrived back at my brother's apartment. All I wanted to do was collapse. The people, the heat, the noise, the cranky complaints about the day, and all the travel combined with the difficult months of the depression had drained my strength. I had nothing left to give anyone.

Charlie made an insulting remark, and his words triggered a reaction in me that precipitated the first fight we had had in several months. I flew into a rage. I could tell by the intensity of my response that I needed a major time-out. For years, we had had a policy in place whereby either of us had the privilege of leaving an argument if we noticed that we were moving into the destructive zone. I was so anxious to leave the apartment that I didn't stop to put my sandals back on. I just picked them up and rushed toward the door.

Then Charlie did something he had never done before and has never done since. He blocked my way, standing squarely in front of the door. Some vicious, aggressive killer instinct emerged from my shadows, and I started beating him in the face with my leather sandals. All three children were watching their normally self-controlled mother go berserk. Charlie stepped aside, and I escaped into downtown Manhattan.

It was a very important moment in my life. Briskly walking the streets of New York, I began to calm down. I didn't feel a bit guilty. I just felt sad about how far I had fallen. I found some compassion for myself for having put out so much energy to so many people for so long. I realized that under prolonged, stressful circumstances, with enough provocation, I was capable of causing physical harm even to those I loved.

When I finally returned to my brother's apartment, I was calm enough to patch things up by apologizing for my violent outburst, and Charlie apologized for standing in the doorway. The children were still awake and observed each of us acknowledging our part in the breakdown.

The next day, we returned home exhausted and depleted by our "vacation." The load I had been carrying for six months had started catching up with me. I was beginning to unravel and was worn thin. I needed a break—from the house, from the kids, from work, and especially from supporting Charlie. I was on duty pretty much round the clock. Charlie hated to disturb me and had taken to leaving the bedroom when his tormented sleep woke him in the middle of the night. At least two or three times a week, he would either unintentionally or deliberately wake me with the hope of making some contact that might dispel the demons attacking him.

Sleep deprivation had compounded his depression and made my life more difficult. It also contributed to his having a panic attack a few days after our return. I called a friend who suggested I get a psychiatric referral from our meditation teacher. I did and Charlie started seeing another doctor. Seymour put Charlie on a different medication, and he began to sleep better at night, so I could too.

I felt that things were improved enough that I could take a week away and go on a meditation retreat with Thich Nhat Hanh. Charlie assured me that he was strong enough to handle the children for my much-needed rest away from home, but I had my doubts. I was afraid to go because he still seemed so fragile. I felt that leaving him for the week was dangerous, but I knew how much I needed this break. I decided to trust Charlie's encouragement to go and tore myself away.

When I got to the retreat at Mount Madonna, the sheer physical beauty of the setting was awe-inspiring. I spent all my breaks in the forest surrounding the center, feeling comforted by the trees. Being with this holy man was inspiring. I felt so nourished to be with such a wise spiritual teacher for an entire week. I felt honored to walk right beside him during walking meditation.

My racked nervous system had a chance to calm down. This master's teachings were strong reinforcement for those I had learned from Jack Kornfield and Stephen Levine. The foundation of my belief system containing mindfulness, compassion, and loving-kindness were fortified for the challenges I would be returning to. I managed my intense anxiety that erupted when I called home. It was a huge challenge to be with my fears that Charlie could suicide while I was away. Despite the distress that I heard in Charlie's voice during our phone connections, I managed, with great effort, to not be pulled into the anguish that he was experiencing at home. I was able to complete the retreat and to obtain the relief and restoration I had hoped for. I came home restored. When I returned, the house was a huge mess, but it didn't bother me because everyone was alive, and they were all happy to see me. But most importantly, I felt that I had fuel in my tank to go the next distance.

Not long after my retreat I was reassured by seeing Charlie responding to the medications and sleeping better at night. In October, an old friend invited Charlie to bicycle from San Francisco to Los Angeles along the Pacific Coast Highway. Charlie had never ridden his bicycle more than twenty miles at a time, much less four hundred, but he agreed to do it. I was sick with worry that after all we'd been through, he was going to die in a biking accident. I was in a state of tension all week until they arrived home safely. Charlie came home looking fit, his self-confidence and life force back, the depression completely gone. I rejoiced.

Charlie was so delighted to be alive and to feel a sense of purpose again. His heart was open, and his eyes were bright. He was back! In the next few months the network grew considerably, our reputation was spreading, and we were once again, enjoying our work. We were learning where each other's strengths and talents lay and utilizing them. We were sharing power well, and enjoying harmony and well-being. The kids were beginning to show signs of playfulness and affection, and our house was feeling like a home for the first time in a long time. It seemed too good to be true. And yet it was true, for the time being.

Chapter 19

HITTING BOTTOM AND COMING UP

Charlie

By late summer, the load Linda had been carrying for six months caught up with her. She was worn thin and needed a break—from the house, kids, work, and especially me. She was on duty pretty much round the clock. To avoid disturbing her, I had taken to leaving the bedroom when my tormented sleep woke me in the middle of the night, but despite my efforts, at least two or three times a week I would wake Linda, unintentionally or deliberately, with the hope of making some contact that might dispel the demons attacking me.

Out of necessity over the past months, I had been taking a back seat to her in our workshops. As I felt more isolated, more depressed, and more anxious, the idea of being seen in a public setting like our seminars and risking exposure of the inner pain I could no longer conceal was becoming an increasingly terrifying possibility. I was barely functional. I could only be a hindrance and an embarrassment to Linda, who, by now, was quite comfortable in her new role of lead facilitator. "Once people see what kind of shape I'm in," I told Linda, "it will only be a matter of time before the word gets out to the public, and there goes our reputation."

Linda tried to get me to see things differently. "You don't look to others the way you feel inside. Most people don't even know anything is going on, and those who do just think you're working out some midlife stuff." She reminded me that many of the people signed up for the workshop were ex-students of mine coming largely to be with me and that they would be very disappointed if I didn't show up. But the main thing that Linda wanted me to see was that together we could do it.

Quietly and clearly, she reminded me that I could and would rise to the occasion when I had to. "Have you considered the possibility that maybe your presence is needed in the workshop to teach something other than what you think you're there to teach?" she asked. "Maybe what these men need to know is that you don't have to keep it together all the time, that it's okay to be shaky, to be dependent, to lean on a woman once in a while; that a man can still be a man and be vulnerable or scared; that you can drop the posturing and pretense and still be worthy of respect—in fact, be worthier of respect—because you're being real and authentic in your pain. For God sakes, somebody's got to show these guys that a man doesn't have to be strong all the time! Look what it does to the ones who keep trying! It killed your father, and it's killing you, and it's killing a lot of the men who are going to be in the workshop this weekend. Maybe you're being so untogether is exactly what they need to see, to know that a man can be worthy of love and respect even when he's not strong."

In August Linda registered for a meditation retreat on the central coast of California led by Thich Nhat Hanh, a Vietnamese Buddhist monk who, for several years, had been an inspirational teacher to us both. She was counting the days until she would leave for the retreat. Although I knew Linda desperately needed to go, I was apprehensive about her leaving. Whenever she was out of my sight for long, I would start to feel anxious. For someone used to spending weeks on the road without getting homesick, this was quite a change. During the rare times when I was able to, I joked with Linda about her finally having her dream come true: she had me all to herself, all the time. I reminded her of Oscar Wilde's famous statement: "There are only two real tragedies in life. One is not getting what you really want and the other is getting it." In this case she had gotten it, but it wasn't exactly what she had in mind.

As much as I hated and was terrified by the idea, for the sake of her sanity, I knew that Linda needed to put some distance between us and replenish her depleted energy. I told her not to worry, that I would be fine, though I knew that she knew that it was false bravado. Linda's trip confronted me with the lack of support in my life. I had put most of my energies into my work, directing the little that was left to my family. With little inclination and less energy to support the development of close male friendships, I had isolated myself, attached to the belief that one's spouse should be sufficient to fulfill all personal and relational needs.

On the morning of her departure, I helped Linda load her car and kissed her goodbye. Within moments of her leaving, I was flooded with anxiety. My mind went wild with accusative and catastrophic thoughts. "You won't be able to manage the kids. Jesse will get arrested or worse. You'll become suicidal. Linda's care is the only thing that's kept you from losing it and now she's gone. It's all over. You never should have let her go. You need a babysitter or you won't survive." I couldn't imagine how I would ever be able to make it through the week when minutes after Linda drove away, I was already a wreck.

I struggled to remind myself that my thoughts did not accurately reflect the reality of my situation. They were simply like raving children who had been badly hurt and who were lashing out in desperation and fear. I remembered Jack's reminder that what I stood to gain from all this suffering was greater compassion for myself and for others.

Those words helped keep the wild thoughts from eating me alive. I prayed for enough breathing room to make it through the week. I had rarely ever prayed before. My fixation on hyper-independence saw dependence even on God as a weakness.

Quite unintentionally, I found myself seeking solace from an unfamiliar place that seemed to represent my only chance of surviving the week. I prayed that I would make it, that the kids would be okay that Linda would find the replenishment she so desperately needed and come home restored.

Despite my prayers, the week did not go well. I was obsessively preoccupied with my internal struggle with the demons and had very little energy or attention to give to the kids. I went through the motions, mechanically doing what I could, repeatedly telling them that I wasn't feeling well, and hoping that they would magically stop needing me. They didn't, and the fighting and outbursts continued unabated. Without Linda's intervention, things became worse than ever. Hating the sounds of the kids' relentless arguing, yelling, and crying, I felt powerless to intervene and, for the most part, simply sat there, at the kitchen table or on the living room couch, helplessly waiting for it to end, saying nothing, doing nothing.

On one occasion, I couldn't restrain myself and exploded in a frenzy of rage at Sarah, whose incessant whining had pushed me over the edge. I grabbed her, screaming, "Stop it! Stop it!" Naturally, she burst into hysterical crying, having never gotten such a response from me before. It was and still is the only time I had ever touched her in anger—a clear indicator that I was well over the edge.

The nights were the worst. I was rarely exhausted enough to fall sleep before one o'clock, and after perhaps two or three hours of fitful sleep, I was awake for good, eyes open, mind raging, heart racing, too tired to get out of bed, too tense and wired to go back to sleep. The four-hour wait until dawn seemed interminable.

On the third day of her retreat, Linda called. I wanted to be strong enough on the phone to reassure her that she needn't worry. I did not want to spoil her retreat. No such luck. My body and mind were too beaten and exhausted to hide my desperation. Interlacing my misery with apologies, I spilled it out all over her, hating my weakness as I did. Linda listened, comforting me as best she could. I clung to her, not wanting the conversation to end and simultaneously wanting to free her. Finally, mercifully, we ended the call. For a few moments, I hadn't felt desperately alone and empty. That was over now; just four more days to go. It might as well have been an eternity.

The kids and I managed to survive the week, but I was a wreck by the time Linda came home. Although she had found some replenishment during her time away, she returned to find me clingier and more desperate than when she had left. It took me less than a week to suck out of her the energy she had gained. Now no break was in sight for either of us.

A week later, Linda called a friend asking for a referral to a psychiatrist who could prescribe some medication for me. She rightly reasoned that if things didn't turn around soon, we were both going to end up in the hospital. Linda took me to the appointment. When I met the doctor, my initial impression was "This is a caring man."

"What can I do for you?" he asked, and the sincerity behind his simple question moved me literally to tears. He really did want to do something for me!

After listening to me and then to Linda pour out our thoughts and feelings, he confirmed that I was seriously depressed—Really?—and in need of medication, immediately. He asked if I would be willing to see one of his colleagues, a specialist in depression and psychopharmacology. I agreed.

Five days later, Linda and I drove to San Francisco, and once again I found myself sitting in a medical office awaiting a diagnosis and treatment. The doctor was cool, objective, and scientifically detached in a comforting sort of way. After I completed a psychiatric inventory, he informed me that I was profoundly depressed and that most people in the shape I was in were heavily medicated, hospitalized, or both. He told us that I probably didn't require hospitalization but that I would need to be medicated. The questions, of course, were which meds and how much. "Given your symptoms and the likelihood of a hereditary factor in your father's psychiatric history, it's probable you'll find some relief with lithium."

"You mean it's probable that I'm manic-depressive?"

He danced around my question, refusing to answer it directly, but the gist of what I heard was, "Of course, dummy! What the hell else could it mean? Who else takes lithium?" Strangely enough, I felt relieved. True, my worst fears were being confirmed, almost. Still, the possibility that lithium could turn this thing around before I really went crazy was enough to give me some hope.

I asked if I would have to be on lithium for the rest of my life if it worked. The doctor did a little more dancing, but his answer essentially was "yes." I would probably need to be maintained on lithium to keep the manic-depression under control. Three months before, I would have preferred being roasted over a spit to being dependent on a drug to keep me from falling apart. Now all I could muster was a weak "Okay."

I filled the prescription that same day and began the countdown of days when I could expect to experience a shift in my mood. I had been warned that it could be several weeks or even longer before I would notice anything and that, even then, there was no guarantee. I secretly hoped that I would be different from the average patient and would experience amazing results right away. That did not prove to be the case.

While the meds did help to improve my sleep, they didn't do much to reverse my deeply negative mood. My weekly meetings with Seymour, my new psychiatrist, were costing us several hundred dollars a month, money we didn't have. But if therapy might have even a chance of helping me, I had to do it. Somehow, we would manage to come up with the money.

Meanwhile, Linda and I continued to schedule relationship courses in several different cities, and by now she was doing them on her own with increasing frequency. I just wasn't up to it. Although I hated her traveling as much as she did, I was grateful that the students kept coming even when only one of us showed up to teach. If I couldn't work, then I could at least try to hold down the fort while she went out and brought in some income.

Our role reversal was now complete. I was the depressed househusband who had dinner ready for his wife when she came home from work and carried her bags into the house when she returned from a trip.

Two months after getting on the meds, I still wasn't out of the depression. I was, however, no longer sinking deeper into it, and at times, I even saw a slight glimmer of light that signaled I might someday be out of the tunnel. Convinced that this was the case, I still believed that the forty-five minutes a week with my therapist was the best possible way for me to spend my time and money. What he gave me, in addition to his encouraging support and understanding, was the acceptance and compassion I had never received from another man and had never been able to give myself.

Like so many other men, my lack of connection with my father had left me with a wound that no amount of love from Linda could heal. Without an authentic male connection, I would be doomed to endlessly play out approval-seeking cycles in hopes that one day I would finally earn the magic blessing that would make me whole.

In Seymour, I had found a man who was both strong and loving. He was able to accept my suffering and pain without pity or judgment. From him, I learned how to be compassionate. I learned that love is not necessarily soft and syrupy but can be firm, clear, and strong. I came to understand what it means to truly respect myself. I saw that only by respecting myself would I be able to truly respect others. I learned what responsibility really means, and that it has nothing to do with blame, duty, guilt, or obligation. I was able to appreciate more fully that when there is suffering, one of the things that people most need is for someone with sufficient strength and caring to listen intently to them. I learned that it is out of the quality of that listening that healing occurs, not from advice or feedback.

I was slowly beginning to trust myself, learning that I didn't have to be a slave to the relentless demands of my ego, which never had been and probably never would be satisfied with my best efforts. I was beginning to understand that who I am is enough and that I don't have to embellish my public image with noble achievements, great accomplishments, or evidence of extraordinariness. I learned that being nobody special was really all right and that accepting the possibility that being ordinary was not a sin or a failure. I began to see how practically everything I had ever done was motivated by a desire for the validation and acknowledgment I'd hoped would fill the void in my soul that I had compulsively denied.

As I worked my therapy in the coming months, these things became clearer to me. And as they did, the depression gradually began to lift. It wasn't just the insights and illuminations that emerged in our sessions that slowly cleared away the heaviness of my despair; it was the experience of being seen openly and completely, stripped of the image props and accessories without which I had previously never left home. It wasn't just in being seen naked that granted me a sense of dignity and validity; it was that Seymour was qualified to bestow the blessing I needed, not because of his position in society as a highly respected professional but by virtue of his tremendous capacity to give love.

In late October, my friend Michael, persuaded me to bike the Pacific Coast Highway with him from San Francisco to Los Angeles. I had never ridden a bike more than twenty miles and was in no condition to do a four-hundred-mile trip. Michael insisted that I *could* do it despite my doubts. One hour into the trip I had to pull over, exhausted and certain that he was wrong. "I'm sorry, Michael," I pleaded. "We've barely begun, and I'm already whipped. I never should have agreed to do this. I agreed because I wanted to keep my word about our agreement and I didn't want to disappoint you. I was hoping that by some miracle I'd be able to do it. I was wrong, and I'm sorry. You can continue if you want, but I've got to go home now."

"I know that you think that you can't do this. I've been there myself. Many times. Here's what I think will help. I'm going to let you take the lead. You be the front rider and set the pace and I'll follow. I don't care if it takes us a month to get to L.A. You can determine when we take breaks. As often as you want. I guarantee you that if you go at the pace that is most comfortable for you, that will be fine with me, and you'll make it. You'll see. Just give it a chance. If I'm wrong you can go home."

Exasperated, and convinced that Michael was wrong, I agreed, mainly to get him off my back and expecting to announce that I was going home within the next hour or so. But much to my surprise, but not to Michael's, I didn't. In fact, as the trip progressed, I upped the speed that we were riding at and decreased the frequency and length of our breaks. The trip never got easy. It was challenging all the way to the end, but my strength and confidence grew, and so did my self-respect.

When we rode into L.A., on day seven of the trip, I felt a sense of pride that I hadn't experienced for what seemed like ages. I also felt enormously grateful to Michael for being a true friend and seeing in me what I couldn't see in myself.

I felt like I had turned a corner in making this trip. Continually pressing myself beyond what I had held to be my personal limits; challenging my notions of my own physical, emotional, and mental capabilities; and not succumbing to the tendency to give up, all had a profound impact on me. I was almost violently shaken out of my depression, and the melancholic gloominess that had consumed me for so long had become an unreal memory. The medication that I had stopped taking on the third day of the trip now seemed like a crutch for which I had no further use. I decided not to resume it unless the black hole began to overtake me again. I resisted the impulse to throw away the rest of the pills, though I knew inside that I was finished with them.

We pedaled all the way to the LAX airport and boxed up our bikes before boarding our plane to San Francisco.

As our plane took off and Michael and I watched the City of Angels disappear below us, I felt overcome with elation and then the kind of gratitude that comes from receiving something so deeply desired, one dared not even hope for it. The nightmare was over, and I was on my way home. It was really over. I reached over and took Michael's hand. We both looked at each other and smiled.

Chapter 20

AFTER THE NIGHTMARE

Charlie

Although the early stages of my recovery had been subtle and gradual, things took a dramatic turn after the bike trip. I arrived home energized and inspired to get back to work. I found that my vision of Linda had been transformed as well. I now trusted her at a deeper level than I ever had before. I was certain that the shift in my perception of her had to do with having had a direct experience of her strength and competence.

I had seen many couples resist the disintegration of the structure of their relationship and cling with all their might to an outmoded, dysfunctional model out of fear of losing their connection altogether. Often it turned out that their unwillingness to let go brought about the very thing that they feared the most. Linda and I had been granted the good fortune to be thrust into a circumstance in which holding onto the old pattern was no longer an option, and we had no other choice but to step into the unknown.

It was 1989, and another aspect of the personal empowerment movement was coming into prominence. It became known as the "Men's Movement," and its leaders included prominent writers, poets, philosophers, and psychologists. In late spring I got a call from John, the former head of research and design at the company. He invited me to join him in attending a large gathering of men in San Francisco on the following weekend.

Twenty years my senior, John described himself as a "recovering psychologist." In the late 1960s he'd left his clinical practice to become involved in the fledgling human potential movement. Known for his uncanny ability to spontaneously create group processes in the spur of the moment, John was a masterful designer of experiential exercises. John and I had become close friends almost immediately after he was hired by the company. Among the things that we had in common were our views regarding the "shadow side" of the company. As John became increasingly disenchanted with what he referred to as "the business" he began to disengage, and five months after I left the company, he, too, was gone.

Although I had little interest in being a part of a bunch of drum-beating, chest-thumping guys, John was relentless in his insistence that we find out about all the excitement about the men's movement, so I decided to join him the next weekend. The event featured several leaders of the movement, including the poet Robert Bly and mythologist Michael Meade.

On the morning of the event, we arrived early at the auditorium where hundreds of men were already gathered in front of the building's entrance. At precisely ten o'clock, the doors opened to the sound of thunderous drumbeats. Men wearing animal skins and masks appeared and ushered us all inside. The room vibrated with an almost frightening intensity. Drumming and chanting filled the air. Men leaped up in spontaneous dance. Despite some hesitancy, I joined in, not because I felt obliged to but because the enthusiasm was contagious and felt irresistible. The seemingly chaotic ritual went on for nearly an hour without a word being spoken; then, as if on cue, the celebration of wildness dissolved into stillness and silence.

Almost immediately I began to feel a kind of kinship with all the men surrounding me. I hadn't experienced anything like it before, and for the first time in my life, I felt a deep connection with other men. I no longer felt I was with strangers, and the guard that usually automatically went up when I found myself in unfamiliar situations, dissolved.

That day was filled with a quality of caring, support, and nurturing that was unfamiliar to me. We shared feelings, longings, fears, pain, and dreams that many of us had never outwardly acknowledged. The ego-tripping, posturing, and protective games that so frequently had characterized my relations with men seemed unnecessary and out of place here. I experienced an enormous sense of freedom and relief that came from acknowledging the fear of being judged as inadequate by other men and the need to compensate for this "deficiency" or conceal it in shame. The power that came from recognizing our common experience was exhilarating. In a matter of hours, we penetrated the protective roles that bred the disease of isolationism, from which so many of us had suffered.

At the day's end, I had a very different sense of myself and of my place in the male community. I had an awareness that my struggles were more universal, even archetypal, and less personal. In hearing the deeper truth of other men, I saw the wounds that we suffer living in a culture that views human beings in terms of utilitarian value. Although I had intellectually understood this before, I hadn't known it on a gut level, as I did now. I felt a different kind of connection from that shared by men in side-by-side activities such as work, sports, or combat. This was a soulful union that dissolved the barriers keeping us separate from the truth in our own hearts and the hearts of others.

The men's gathering was as illuminating for John as it was for me. We each realized that what most men need is what both of us needed and got during the gathering: a place to come together with other men where we can let down our guard, masks, and roles and speak and hear the truth of each other's experience. A place where we can begin to see the bigger picture and begin to free ourselves of the shame and blame inherent in not being able to live up to the impossible male stereotype so many of us strive futilely to embody.

Our drive home was filled with an outpouring of questions, ideas, and possibilities. If a thousand men could have such a profound experience in a one-day retreat, what might be possible with a smaller group over a longer time? What would it require to set up the conditions that would allow for a group to go even deeper than we had? Were we qualified to set up such a group, and if we did would anyone be interested in attending?

Ten days after the gathering, John and I went to the Esalen Institute in Big Sur for a brainstorming retreat. At the end of three days, we had a design for an experiential retreat for men focusing on recovery from the damaging elements of our social conditioning. We called it "Man to Man." The following week we scheduled a weekend at a Northern California retreat center and invited several dozen men from the Bay Area, as well as other parts of the country.

The turnout was much greater than either of us had expected, and the weekend exceeded our greatest hopes. John was easy and fun to co-facilitate with, and it felt good to work with another man after having spent so much of the past three years working primarily with Linda. John and I could play and easily bounce off each other in ways that Linda and I couldn't. Yet the workshop had great depth.

Word about Man to Man spread quickly, and within a few months we had facilitated retreats in several cities and scheduled several more. It felt great to have another event to offer, particularly one that was so personally gratifying and relevant to my concerns at the time. I could not only begin to relax my worries about finances a little, but I could also begin to spend some work time apart from Linda.

It felt like the pendulum had swung too far in the direction of togetherness, and having spent so much time living and working closely with Linda, I had more than made up for the years in which we had spent so much time apart. I was ready to strike a different kind of a balance, one in which we had more diversity in our work and personal lives.

The antagonism that had characterized the kids' behavior and their relationships with each other was now significantly diminished, and for the first time in years, our house was starting to feel like a home again. We had moved into what we referred to as the "post-chaos" stage of life.

In addition to restructuring our personal lives, Linda and I also made some changes in our professional lives. We redesigned our couples' workshop and made it available to singles as well. Contact people in several cities were now promoting seminars and enrolling people for us. We usually averaged two workshops a month, and because they were only two days each, we had plenty of time left for the kids and other family-related activities. For the first time since we'd moved to California, we even had time for a garden, an indicator that we had moved beyond survival and into a mode in which we were thriving.

In the spring of 1989, Paula, a former student, called me from Salt Lake City and asked if I would teach a course there. The arrangement would be that I would design and facilitate a workshop on conscious living, Paula would promote it, and we would split the profits. After several conversations, we came up with a plan, and in two weeks I had developed another course for our growing network. I called it "Waking Up," and it was the first seminar that I had designed and would facilitate completely by myself.

By late summer I had facilitated two courses in Salt Lake City, with more scheduled for several other cities. Between Waking Up, Man to Man, and Empowering Relationships, I suddenly found myself as busy with work and travel as I had been at the company. What was different this time was I was the one making the decisions about where and when I would work.

Another difference was that Linda and I were truly connected with each other in a way that we were not before.

When we were together, we were together. Her life was fuller than it had been before, and both of us could give more to each other and to the kids. We checked in with each other daily to see how things were going and made whatever adjustments to our schedules that were needed to keep things balanced.

We had hit a peak in our relationship. Our personal and professional needs were all being met, and the whole family was beginning to thrive. We were anticipating a future that would be free of the kind of painful adversity that had characterized so much of the previous several years. We had endured a great deal, but we had also grown and learned a lot, and we were stronger at the broken places. It seemed that we would never be at risk of repeating the mistakes of the past, and so we had no need to worry about going too far this time. Our trust with each other and ourselves was stronger than it had ever been. This wasn't just wishful thinking; it was the truth, the real deal. Or so it seemed.

Chapter 21

MEDITATING ON THE EDGE OF THE WELL

Linda

On January 19, 1991, I woke up gasping and panicky from a vivid dream in which I had felt a hard, little lump in my left breast. Upon waking, I immediately felt the spot where the lump was and found that there was, indeed, a literal lump. When I saw my OBGYN two days later, as soon as she touched the lump, she said, "This is a bad one. I'm going straight to the phone to call the surgeon for an appointment for you." At the end of the week I found myself sitting with Charlie, in a small examining room waiting to hear the results of a fine needle biopsy that I had just had at the University of California San Francisco Medical Center. After sitting in nervous silence for about twenty minutes, the physician, Dr. Goodson came into the room holding some papers looking serious and somewhat grim. "I'm afraid the news isn't good. The tumor is malignant."

With his pronouncement, I immediately became filled with terrifying thoughts and questions: "How much time do I have left?" was my first thought. It was followed, unanswered, by a flood of other thoughts none of which I was able to actually express. They all seemed to come at once. "Is this really happening? Am I still in that dream? How can this be? But I've tried so hard to be a good person. Am I being punished? Have I done something wrong? I don't deserve this. No, I'm not ready to go. I'm not done yet. The kids still need me. I'm too young. I'm not ready to die!"

The ride home was cold and rainy, and we were both so numb that we could barely speak. When I got home, I began the grief process. All the people I had known with cancer were much older than me. My belief at the time was that you get diagnosed and then die soon afterward. I saw myself laid out in a coffin with grieving relatives and friends at my funeral saying, "She was only forty-four; such a tragedy. So young!"

I cried out my sadness about not seeing the children grow up. I wanted to be a part of their development, to love them and teach them the things I consider to be important about life. When I imagined myself dead, I felt at peace knowing how devoted a father Charlie had become. We had gotten the kids off to a good start, and Charlie was definitely up to the job of caring for them well. I hated the thought of missing the unfolding of who they would become, even though I was confident that they would turn out well.

I grieved for the years I feared I might not have. There were so many things I had looked forward to that I could be robbed of, being a grandmother, being there for Charlie when he got old and sick, being a wise old woman who, having experienced so much in life, could open my heart in compassion and to be a great resource for others. I imagined that people would come to me for counseling and classes and in friendship to learn. It's so hard to let go of hopes and expectations of the future, maybe even harder than letting go of the past.

I imagined that the cancer had already spread throughout me. Every physical symptom magnified, from the burning sensation in my back to the infected pierce holes in my ear lobes to my fatigue became evidence that the cancer was rampant and about ready to kill me.

I had been asking myself all day long, "Is this the worst day of my life?" Yet by that evening, I realized that it wasn't. I had

had lots of days much worse than this one. Ugly, old memories from many years before were being triggered. Compared to the times that we had been so painfully disconnected, and I felt utterly alone, this was bad but preferable. Many people think I'm a nut and have trouble understanding how these times in the past when Charlie and I were so disconnected that divorce seemed imminent were more devastating to me than hearing that I had cancer. But it's true.

The archetype that lives and breathes in me is the Greek goddess Hera, the wife. All my life, what I've wanted more than anything is to be married and create a great love and a beautiful family. For my marriage to fail was the greatest horror for me, worse even than facing death. What kept it from being the worst was that Charlie and I were close, physically, emotionally, and spiritually, every moment of this momentous day.

The psychic devastation I experienced when the marriage was failing was infinitely more traumatic for me than having a life-threatening illness. The years Charlie worked for the company were dreadful because I felt so utterly alone. In contrast, even if the very worst were true, I knew that I would never be alone like that again. I was frightened, but I knew that I was deeply loved.

I viewed Charlie's reaction to my cancer diagnosis as if he were a frightened little boy, clutching Mommy's skirt. He held on to me all day long, both in fear of losing me and in his desire to provide me with his strength. He seemed more frightened of my dying than I was.

The cancer tore both of our hearts open. I was raw and from the moment of the diagnosis everything in life was more vivid. The light was brighter, colors were more intense, feelings were more poignant, people were more beautiful, and love was fuller and deeper. I felt more alive than ever before, so I cried out my sadness about imagining my life's work aborted. I was startled by the intensity of the despair around being prevented by death from writing books and teaching couples what I had so painstakingly learned.

But I had immediate business to attend to. There was a pressing urgency to decide about treatment. We had a lot to learn quickly and big, important decisions to be made at a time when I was feeling overwhelmed and frightened. Within two weeks of my own breast cancer diagnosis, two of my friends, both women in my age group who also lived in Sonoma, were diagnosed with breast cancer. We had to make decisions about our treatment. They both decided to have lumpectomies but refused radiation and chemotherapy.

Preferring natural to chemical healing myself, I also was not inclined to go the chemotherapy and radiation route. For years we had lived in the country and had cultivated a huge organic garden and had frozen and canned vegetables. Our second child, Eben, was home born. I had breastfed for five years (total for the three children) and shopped in health food stores. Spiritual healing was at the core of my professional work with clients and my seminars.

I spent time reading medical articles and speaking with women who had breast cancer. Ultimately, I left no stone unturned. This would not be an either/or choice. I would go with both Eastern and Western medicine. I decided to hit the cancer with everything I could.

The surgery did not cause me serious distress. Unlike some women, I did not feel cut up, intruded on, violated, or mutilated. To me, having the malignant tumor and lymph nodes removed surgically was like suctioning mucous from a newborn baby's throat so she can take her first breath of air and live. I was also lucky to have a surgeon I trusted and liked. Radiation was time-consuming but not difficult. I sailed through the thirty-three treatments with little problem.

Chemotherapy, on the other hand, was a nightmare. My doctor was cold and businesslike. I didn't like her, and I didn't trust her. Not having a good relationship with her made the whole experience infinitely worse. But the doctors couldn't say for sure whether the cancer was anywhere else in my body, so I submitted to being voluntarily poisoned.

When I was so sick and weak from the chemo that I couldn't work or do much of anything except just vegetate in bed, imagining dying was easy. I could see my body deteriorating to the point where I didn't have enough life force left and my spirit being forced to leave it. I flashed on scenes of my memorial service and then quickly jumped ahead in time to Charlie becoming involved with another woman. She was younger, slimmer, prettier, and healthier than me. I could see her shoes in the bottom of my closet and her clothes hanging where mine used to be. Her toiletries were on the bathroom sink, and her toothbrush in the same cup with Charlie's. I pictured the two of them talking intimately in our big bed and looking into each other's eyes when they made love.

Jealousy has been an issue for me all my life, but this was a new challenge: managing jealousy of the woman who would replace me after I died. These two parts struggled within me: the petty, possessive side who preferred Charlie remain alone and true to my memory vying with my greater, generous self who just wanted him to be happy.

Lying in bed, I alternated between thinking that maybe I had no cancer in my system and was going through this horrible discomfort unnecessarily and fearing that the chemotherapy might not get all the cancer and that I would end up dead despite everything.

Keeping a cheerful, optimistic attitude when I felt so terrible and didn't have the strength to engage in my normal activities like working, exercising, and even talking to friends were difficult. Some days, I was too sick to even listen to a tape, and I would just lie in bed for hours, aching all over, anticipating my death. On top of all this, I felt ashamed that I had gotten cancer. I couldn't get away from the notion that I had done something wrong and that cancer was my punishment.

I was continually plagued by the question, "Why?" I kept thinking that if I could discover a satisfactory explanation, I'd find some peace. Every week I would come up with a new explanation. First, it was fat in the diet. Japanese women who have a very low incidence of cancer don't eat much fat. I became convinced that I had overindulged, that too many hamburgers and potato chips when I was younger had given me breast cancer. The second week, I clung to the explanation of immune system suppression because of stress and having previously done work that I really didn't enjoy.

Then I became convinced that the cause was genetic because my mother, as well as several other relatives on both sides of my family, had died of cancer. The doctors never found the site of origin for my mom's cancer. It had already metastasized to her liver by the time she was diagnosed. This theory was very appealing because it took a lot of pressure off me. I didn't have to be ashamed. I couldn't do anything about heredity. It wasn't my fault.

In week four, I thought it was drugs. My doctor had mentioned that the San Francisco Bay Area had the highest incidence of breast cancer of anywhere in the United States. He stated that alcohol consumption is also higher in the Bay Area than elsewhere in the country and speculated that there might be a relationship there. The alcohol theory didn't have any applicability to me since I don't even average a glass of wine per month. I was left feeling guilty about the psychedelic drugs that I had ingested during the sixties. Maybe they had damaged my body and made me vulnerable to cancer.

In the fifth week, I became convinced that it was the high-dose estrogen birth control pills I took in my late teens and early twenties, the first ones to come out, had finally caught up with me. During week six, I reverted to the lowered immune system because of stress theory with a new twist. This particular week, I was desperately seeking someone other than myself to blame, and I chose Charlie. I became convinced that the pain created by his being away from the family for so many years had created enough stress to start up a cancerous tumor. This theory made as much sense as any of the others. I didn't share it with Charlie, however. I might be wrong, and he would only feel guilty.

I became convinced that I was a canary in the mine and that my cancer was a result of the polluted environment. My sensitive system had left me more vulnerable to the toxins in the air, water, and food. I wanted a straightforward explanation for how I had gotten cancer in the first place so I wouldn't have to feel so despairing and powerless. I could really understand why people would want to latch on to a particular theory. For instance, if you attach to the fat in the diet theory, you can go on a macrobiotic or McDougal's diet and rest easy that you've got cancer handled. But none of the theories really worked for me. I concluded that there was a constellation of factors and that medical science is still guessing.

My friends and family really came through for me during this time. They visited, sent cards, letters, books, and tapes and left loving messages on the answering machine. People from all over the country, some of whom I didn't even know, were praying for my recovery. Charlie became a most incredible supporter. He was doing everything—taking care of the children, running the business and seeing some of my clients on the days I was too sick from chemotherapy to work. He was attentive in ways he had never been before.

When I was so sick from chemotherapy, too weak to get out of bed, the children took turns being close to me. Jesse and Eben would sit on the bed and talk to me, and ten-year-old Sarah would lie next to me and snuggle close. The wave of love I received during my months of treatment lifted me up and carried me through it. Sadness came in waves. The most difficult part of all was the realization that Charlie and I were not likely to grow old together. I had assumed that I would lay my hands on his aching joints and support and comfort him in his aging and dying.

Realizing that I might not have an old age at all forced me to embrace my spirituality in a whole new way. Recognizing that my physical frailty would eventually force me to drop my body made me acutely aware that I needed to develop my spiritual self. During this time, I read every book I could find about NDEs (near-death experiences) and was struck by how remarkably similar they all were. Reading these accounts helped me to trust that I could have a connection with the eternal part of myself. My developing belief system allowed me to trust that I could support and encourage those whom I loved from the spirit realm. I had more peace knowing that I could create a love so deep that I would never be separated from them.

When the chemotherapy finally ended and I was up and around again, I went through a period of being jealous of almost everyone I saw. Back in aerobics class, I looked at each person in the mirror and thought, "They don't have cancer, and I do." I was envious of their vibrant good health. I was envious of Charlie's strong body and his stamina.

An important part of my learning has been accepting that the cause of my cancer had no clear explanation. This recognition has helped me to live with the ambiguity and mystery that characterize so much of life. It's been tough for me to live with so much unknown. With no clear cause or cure for breast cancer, I live with Damocles' sword poised over my head, knowing that a reoccurrence is possible at any time. It's frightening, and at the same time, that knowledge keeps me awake to the preciousness of life.

Living so constantly in the presence of the unknown opened me up like nothing else. The cancer propelled me into the awakened state that people meditate for years to attain. I found myself speaking my mind in areas where I might have previously held back. My attitude had become "What the hell difference does it make, even if someone gets flustered or riled?" In the face of death, interpersonal risks shrink in size.

My work has always been very important to me, but after the cancer, it became even more so. When I was well enough to go back to work, I did so with a sense of acute gratitude. I lived with the consciousness that this challenge was sent to me so that I would learn to take better care of my body and teach others to do the same. I was also receiving the lesson of suffering, with fear of death and all the other feelings of guilt, anger, and jealousy, to more fully understand the suffering of others.

In my efforts to discover the factors that might have contributed to my illness, I came to see that fear about not having enough money has been a source of worry throughout much of my life. From an early age, I had learned to be very careful with money. Both my parents grew up in the slums of New York during the Depression. There were times when there was no food on the table, and they had been scarred by the experience and became obsessed with having "enough." I always balance my checkbook and know how much is left in the account. I know exactly how much we make per month and how much we spend.

When I made up my mind to free myself of worry, I realized that before cancer I had resigned myself to living out the remainder of my life as a worrier. I carried the belief that there are two kinds of people—worriers and nonworriers—and since we are born either as one or the other, we can't do much to change. Cancer helped me to see the absurdity of that belief and helped free me from yet another source of the fear I had been carrying.

I became more willing to give to myself. I began to work less and only took on work that I enjoyed. I hired an administrative assistant so I could focus on designing and delivering courses and seeing clients, the creative parts of my work. Lo and behold, when I stepped out of my overly responsible role, Charlie picked up some of the responsibility that I had laid down. Ironically, although our bills had never been higher—because I had no insurance coverage that year, my medical bills exceeded our total income—my fear and worry about money had never been lower. I realized that worry is a moment-to-moment choice and that I have some control over how much of it I do.

I trust that our necessities will be handled and that we will always be able to serve and teach in some form. It may not always look the way I thought, but accepting that is part of trusting.

The year following my cancer diagnosis and treatment was the most creative period of my life. Something about the cancer experience and facing death activated my creative juices in a way that nothing else ever had. During the year following my diagnosis, Charlie and I designed and delivered five new seminars and twelve evening talks that we had professionally taped. Fearing that this might be the last year of my life, I felt compelled to share everything I had learned over the years. I lived in a state of heightened awareness and euphoria during most of that time, just happy to be alive. Every little thing seemed like a blessing. At times I actually felt guilty for enjoying my life so much. Charlie was more devoted to me than he had ever been.

We made time to make love during the day. I gave my best energy to intimacy and sexuality because closeness with Charlie was at the top of my priority list. Work had to take a back seat and make room for the most important parts of my life. I chaperoned every one of the children's field trips and let myself be one of the kids on the outings. I took more time to talk to my kids about what was going on in their lives.

When some of the euphoria eventually—inevitably—faded, I missed the rawness and openness of that time, but my cancer experience permanently and dramatically changed my life. Someone once said, "The greatest healer is the one with a wound that won't heal." Such a wound opens the healer's heart, mind, and spirit in a way that he or she becomes a channel for energies that are not as available to those who do not have such persistent wounds. My wounds opened me to my gifts. Living with metastatic breast cancer, for which there is no cure, is living with the ongoing acute awareness that I really don't know how much time I have left. This awareness is not an intellectual concept but an experiential reality.

One of my teachers once told me a story about his experience in a forest monastery in Burma. He had a very difficult time staying awake during his practice. His teacher told him to meditate sitting on the edge of a well. Doing so solved the problem. Cancer, for me, was like meditating on the edge of the well. It has kept me aware that death is coming and alerts me to the preciousness of life.

Over time, I began to appreciate some of the beauty of cancer. It sounds strange, but in many ways cancer has been a blessing in my life. Living with a keen awareness that there is a limited amount of time makes each day count so much more.

Death came near enough so that I could feel his breath. We communicated without words, only our eyes and body movements. He conveyed to me, "I could take you with me." I responded, "I'm not ready to go with you." He stepped so close that his powerful bulk spoke for itself. "I can take you against your will anytime I choose." I looked directly into his eyes. "I'm not going with you now." He did back away. But having him come so close for that flirtation reminded me that he's never far away.

Chapter 22

THIS CAN'T BE HAPPENING

Charlie

Linda told me about her dream the day after a memorial service for my stepfather who had passed away one week earlier. Her mother had succumbed to cancer nine months earlier. Neither of us imagined that we would have to deal with yet another life-threatening condition. My response to hearing of her dream was to minimize the potential significance of it and attempt to reassure Linda that she had "nothing to worry about." Even when her OBGYN expressed concern, I continued out of my own unwillingness to consider this unspeakable possibility to downplay the likelihood that the lump on her breast could actually be cancerous.

Three days after Linda's OBGYN appointment, we drove to San Francisco to see the surgeon who would biopsy the lump on her breast. We were both hoping and expecting it to be a quick routine visit in which we would be informed that the lump was benign and that would be that.

After sitting together in the waiting room for a half hour, when a nurse came out to take Linda into the examination room, I asked if I could go with her. The nurse begrudgingly agreed. In the tiny, two-seat examination room, we waited again. Linda was, understandably, tense and preoccupied, and my efforts to lighten things up proved less successful than usual.

Twenty minutes later, the Dr. Goodson strode in. He seemed surprised, although not disturbed to see me, brought in another chair, then sat down and delivered, what seemed like a canned talk on the routine exam to follow that would include what would probably be a somewhat painful biopsy. My nervousness had increased during our wait, but I found his businesslike, no-nonsense manner reassuring.

He was right about the biopsy, the part about it being painful. During the insertion and withdrawal of several needles into the small pea-sized growth on her left breast Linda squeezed my hand to the point of nearly cutting off circulation. Having felt useless up to this point, I was glad to be able to provide some support to her.

After the procedure, Goodson left with the sample while we both waited nervously for the results. I knew as soon as he came back to the examining room that something was wrong. "I'm sorry," he began, and that was the last thing I heard distinctly. I struggled during the next thirty-five minutes to pay attention to what he was telling us, but I only heard brief, disconnected fragments of his sentences. "Malignant ... chemo-therapy ... mastectomy ... surgery ... radiation ... tumor ... lumpectomy ... expected duration of survival ...."

I felt removed from the whole scene, more like a bystander than a participant. Competing with my conscious desire to understand what he was saying was a phrase that kept repeating itself in the back of my mind: "This can't be happening." It drowned out everything else.

"Are you all right?" Dr. Goodson suddenly asked, turning to me.

"No, I'm not," I answered weakly, unable to pretend as I thought, "He's basically given my wife a death sentence without the date filled in yet and he asks if I'm okay. Is he for real? Is this for real?"

Less than an hour later, we were driving home in the pouring rain. The whole day had been dark, damp, and cold. The rain seemed appropriate. Linda and I spoke very little during the drive. We were both in shock, and I was catastrophizing the future. Amazingly, the doctor had managed to never mention the actual "C" word.

When we got home, we called the kids into our bedroom and gave them the news. Sarah, at ten, and Eben, at twelve, didn't fully comprehend the implications of the situation, and while we didn't want to keep any secrets from them, we also didn't wish to unnecessarily upset them. Without going into the possible serious consequences of Linda's condition, we let them know that she was going to be getting a lot of medical treatment for a while and that the rest of us would have to rally together to take care of things around the house and give her more support than she had ever needed.

Jesse, almost seventeen, showed more concern than his siblings. He knew that people die from this. Within the last year, both his grandmother and his step-grandfather had, and now his mother might. We all sat on our bed together and tried to speak rationally about a subject that frightened me beyond words.

For the first time since my depression had ended three years earlier, I found myself incapable of providing reassurance and comfort to my children. My mind couldn't let go of the terrible fear that this was the beginning of the end, not just for Linda but for our family as well. Although Dr. Goodson couldn't make any definitive statement about the extent to which the cancer had spread in Linda, he had told us that the lab reports indicated it was a particularly fast-growing malignancy that could, if not quickly eradicated by treatment, go on an unstoppable rampage. He had no answer to the question of what the odds were of getting the cancer out before it was too late.

That night, what I most wanted to provide to the kids and Linda was least possible for me to give: reassurance that everything would be all right. There had been many times when I reassured friends, clients, and students that a crisis was an opportunity. I always seemed to have so many glib responses for people who felt overwhelmed by strong emotions. Suddenly all my words of reassurance rang empty and hollow. I felt cursed, not blessed. I tried to keep the overwhelming thoughts swimming in my brain from spilling out into my family. This is a time, I told myself, for connection, support, and love. It didn't matter that I didn't know what the hell is going to happen. It didn't matter that I had no control over this situation or that I couldn't make everyone or anyone feel better. What matters now is that we can be together.

Amid the frantic horror that enveloped me that night, just hours after leaving the medical center, there was stillness, like the calm found in the eye of a hurricane, a place of peace in which I understood that not having the answers or the reassurance I felt obliged to provide was all right. Being open to whatever was within me, and those around me, was enough. My job now was not to *do* anything but to *be* with the people whom I loved as fully and as completely as possible. Later, I saw that I was still shouldering the burden of being the provider and protector, that, in fact, my identity was still very tied up in those roles. "I thought I had already learned that lesson," I later told a friend. He laughed and reminded me how arrogant believing that we get this stuff completely once and for all was. "We get it; then we forget, and we get it and forget again," he said. "After a while, the lapses of forgetfulness become shorter and less frequent. But that's about as good as it gets for most of us."

Linda's cancer served to remind me of many things that I hadn't even realized I'd forgotten. It made me aware that my worth as a person was not completely contingent on my ability to provide for the needs of others and of how much I loved Linda and how much I wanted her to live. We weren't done with this dance yet. We still had so much more to do and experience together, so much further to go with each other, so much more for us to give and to receive from each other, as well as other people. It wasn't time yet. We were just beginning to learn and teach the real lessons about love and freedom. We were just starting to put our teachings into practice in our own relationship.

That night we went to sleep in each other's arms, and I felt the strength of Linda's grip on my body, as I had at other times when she sought a connection with me. This time I felt no aversion to her tight hold on me. I relaxed into it, feeling grateful that despite feeling inept and helpless, I was giving her something of value just by being fully present with and for her.

It was a while before I fell asleep. I spent a good part of the night doing something I hadn't previously done much of in my life: praying. I prayed for one thing, over and over: enough time to give my love to Linda fully, completely. I wanted to give love so totally that her experience of herself would be transformed and she would see herself as being as beautiful and as unconditionally lovable as I knew she was. The fear I was most consumed by that night was that Linda would die without knowing the full depth of my love. I knew words alone would not be enough to penetrate the walls that I knew still kept her from fully loving and accepting herself. "Just let her live long enough for me to give her this gift; that's all that I ask. Please."

I offered my prayers to whoever or whatever receives the heart's deepest longings. There was nothing I wouldn't have given that night in exchange for the guarantee that this wish would be granted, even my own life. For Linda to die without my giving her what I knew I could, what was rightfully hers, what we had come together to experience would have been tragic. She had gone with me into the pits of my personal hell and had given me a gift that had completely changed my life. Out of the love and devotion in which she bathed me for over a year, I had learned to accept and honor my own life in ways that had never before been possible. She had given me the ability to heal myself. Now it was my turn to give it to her. All I asked for was time.

Nothing concentrates the mind like a cancer diagnosis. I discovered that in a committed relationship, there's no such thing as one person having the illness. While it was Linda who was experiencing the direct assault of the cancer and the treatment, I, too, felt the anxiety, distress, terror, helplessness, guilt, and outrage that accompanies this uninvited guest. Whereas in the past I had found it relatively easy to separate myself emotionally as well as physically from Linda's suffering, that was now impossible. I had told myself that her problems were her problems and if my efforts to help her proved inadequate to change things, then that was just how it was. In other words, I was limited in how involved I would allow myself to be, in how much I would allow myself to care.

Although we had unquestionably come a long way since the painful struggles we experienced during my workaholic years, elements of residual dissatisfaction that occasionally showed up in our relationship leaving one or both of us feeling disconnected. During these times Linda usually was aware of the emotional distance between us. She was almost always the first to bring this disconnect to my attention in an effort to close the gap between us. She found it much easier to remember that when we were closely connected, no problem was insurmountable. When we were not, the slightest upsets seemed impossible to resolve. I still seemed to need a lot of reminders of this fact.

Cancer changed all that. I was stripped of the illusion that I could afford to isolate myself whenever I felt like it. Not knowing how much time we had left together, I was suddenly filled with a sense of urgency that made it impossible for me to withhold myself from Linda. I had been operating as if I had all the time in the world to shut down, not listen, play the right/wrong game, and time to waste. If the cancer had metastasized, which we would know after Linda's surgery, the time we had left could be months—or less. Cancer managed to get my attention like nothing else ever had. I had always believed that if we don't pay attention to the small reminders life gives us to wake up, we would be sent reminders too big to ignore. That belief was no longer just a theory. It was now a reality.

In the days, weeks, and months following Linda's diagnosis, I concentrated on providing whatever support Linda needed to relieve her of as much of her physical and emotional pain as I could, and to deepen the quality of our connection. As it turned out, they were one and the same. What brought relief strengthened our bond. While I could *do* little about the nightmare of cancer treatment, I learned that offering my supportive presence, accepting without resistance or judgment whatever arose, was often enough. I came to understand the sufficiency of simply opening to Linda's fear, pain, rage, or grief without doing anything to try to change her feelings or remove the cause.

My helplessness became the teacher that showed me how to let go of my ingrained tendency to fix, change, stop, or control painful situations. I was reduced to giving Linda the only thing I had left: my loving attention. While I could sometimes help by holding her, wiping her brow, rubbing her back, handling the household responsibilities, often what helped most was to sit or lie with her in silence. I learned about the power of silence: that when we fill the space between us with love, we do more to promote healing than when we fill it with words spoken out of fear and resistance or when we fill it with frantic actions. I learned that the integrity of our connection is the single most important variable in the healing process. I became single-minded in my desire to honor the requirements of that process. In the months ahead, there would be no shortage of opportunities for me to make good on that commitment.

Dr. Goodson had advised Linda to have a lumpectomy to remove the cancerous growth in her breast along with some of her lymph nodes to assess the extent to which the cancer may have metastasized to other parts of her body. He was adamant that this needed to be done immediately. If the cancer had spread to her lymph nodes, surgery would then be followed by several months of intensive chemotherapy after the chemo-therapy; he recommended radiation to eliminate any cancerous cells that might still be present in the breast.

This massive medical assault would take a little more than seven months and would require both Linda and me to put everything else in our lives on the back burner and direct our energies fully to the healing process. The doctor insisted that we make our decision immediately, and he offered no other valid options. We got him to agree to give us a couple of days to consider his strategy and spent that time talking with friends, other doctors, and cancer survivors. We considered alternative, noninvasive forms of healing such as acupuncture and medicinal herbs, as well as more unorthodox forms of treatment that included Mexican health clinics, apricot pit diets, and intensive meditation. In the end, we decided on a treatment route that would include elements of both Eastern and Western healing. Four days after the diagnosis, we gave the doctor the go-ahead to schedule Linda's surgery.

On the following Thursday I drove Linda into San Francisco for the lumpectomy. We were acutely aware that we would know by the end of the day how much of a future we were going to have together. I spent the day in the waiting room. When the surgery was over and Linda in the recovery room still unconscious, Dr. Goodson came out to talk to me. Like the beginning of a bad joke, he told me that there was good news and bad news. The good news was that it looked like they had gotten all the cancer out of Linda's breast and that, as far as he could see, the surgery had been successful. The bad news was that one of her lymph nodes had cancerous cells in it, which meant that it had spread to other parts of her body. How far and to what organs were unknown. The doctor felt that chemo-therapy was now a required, rather than an optional, treatment and that it should be initiated immediately.

One of the things that differentiate cancer cells from noncancerous cells is that they tend to divide very rapidly.

Chemotherapy attempts to stop the spread of these wildly growing cells by destroying them. While it does not always succeed in doing this, it usually succeeds in damaging similar but noncancerous cells that rapidly divide, as in hair follicles and stomach lining. We were told that the chemicals Linda would be taking cause hair loss and severe nausea.

Linda's first chemo appointment was just a few days after her surgery. She was treated in an oncology clinic in Marin County, about a forty-minute drive from our home in Sonoma. The clinic was sterile and antiseptic. Linda was seated in a large vinyl chair and received what we told ourselves was the healing medicine through a needle in her arm. I sat next to her, holding her hand. Despite the feelings of dread that we had both had, I felt strangely at peace, even exhilarated, in my role of supporter to Linda. I was being given my chance to demonstrate my love and commitment, and my gratitude for that opportunity greatly outweighed the trepidation I had over what might follow. Much as I was not particularly looking forward to the sleepless nights, the vomiting, and the baldness that loomed in our immediate future, in a strange way, all that horror was made acceptable, even desirable, because it gave Linda and me a chance to be close, perhaps closer than we had ever been.

I had learned from my depression that the pain that rips us apart also opens our heart to give and receive love in ways that were not previously possible. Within two hours after we returned home, Linda was hit by a massive attack of nausea. It came on suddenly and viciously. Before she had time to make it the fifteen feet from the bed to the bathroom, she was overwhelmed by a spasm of vomiting that literally brought her to her knees. The attacks continued all night, long after her stomach was emptied. The intensity of the gut-wrenching spasms scared us both.

Although the vomiting pretty much subsided after the first night, Linda was almost completely incapacitated for four days. She barely had the strength to get out of bed to go to the bathroom and only was able to force down the smallest bit of bland food. She became nauseated at even the smell of food.

I was Linda's attendant, the kids' caregiver, full-time housekeeper, cook, and chauffeur while trying to maintain some semblance of my work schedule. In addition to my own clients, I even saw a few of Linda's, just to make sure I didn't have too much free time on my hands. My full-time mission was to keep all the plates spinning, to keep it all from falling apart. Though I was working harder, with longer hours and getting less sleep, I was feeling more invigorated and energized than I had felt in years. Rather than feeling overwhelmed and burdened, I felt gratitude and enthusiasm practically every waking moment of the day. I was thankful to have Linda with me and to have an opportunity to serve her and express my love. That far outweighed any difficulties or inconvenience I was experiencing.

Oddly, amid a situation that left me no free time, ease, or relaxation, I felt freer and more at peace than I had in ages. Unconcerned with my own desires and focusing almost exclusively on Linda's needs and those of the children, I had no space to experience the mind states that left me feeling depressed, anxious, or aggravated. In all the years in which I had lectured thousands of students on the virtues of selfless giving, I had never known the truth of those words as vividly as I did at this time.

As a result, I experienced a greater overall sense of wholeness, sufficiency, and worthiness. The catch is that to serve, as a means of filling oneself, is simply another way to take rather than give. God knows I had done more than my share of that. But this was different. I was giving of myself not from a sense of obligation or a desire to fill my own cup but because I was moved to do so in response to an inner feeling of love and gratitude. My giving was not limited to Linda and the kids but extended beyond our family, to my friends, clients, nearly everyone with whom I came in contact.

Each encounter was a gift to me allowing me to press past the limits of my capacity to serve, to find new ways of giving, to attend more fully to each person, to listen more deeply to them, to hear their inner as well as their outer words, to see them with new eyes. I felt like everyone was on my side—an unfamiliar feeling. I usually felt myself to be alone in an unsupportive world, struggling to carry an overwhelmingly heavy burden. At other times, I felt myself to be amid adversaries competing for the scarce resources of money, goods, attention, and love. The more I gave of myself, the more abundant the world felt. The more open and disarmed of defenses I became, the safer I felt.

As Linda began to regain her strength, she resumed a modified version of her pre-chemo life. I continued to carry most of the responsibilities for the family and the business, but she was better able to take care of herself now. This was fine with me since I could catch up with some of the lower priorities that had been dropped by the wayside. I also knew that in three weeks we'd be going through another bout of chemo.

In the meantime, there were plenty of things to take care of. Our insurance company had informed us that Linda was not covered for any of her outpatient treatment, which meant just about all of it since she had spent no time as an inpatient. Now, in addition to having to deal with cancer, we also had the burden of worrying about how to come up with tens of thousands of dollars to cover medical costs. While I did my best to reassure Linda that we would find ways of handling the finances without going bankrupt, inwardly I was furious and scared. This news put a dent in my generally positive spirits, but after explaining the situation to the doctors and hospitals, we came up with payment plans, some of which extended years into the future. I also spoke with several attorneys to find out whether we could sue our insurance company that was threatening to terminate our coverage. It was a long shot, but it was better than rolling over without a fight.

Just as Linda was recovering from her first chemo assault, it was time for the second round. We knew better than to think that the worst was over. Still, we hoped that she could be one of the rare patients whose reaction to chemo diminishes after the first session. Or maybe she would be one of the few who didn't lose her hair.

One of the more maddening aspects of cancer is the tendency of the patient and the patient's loved ones to become obsessed with hope: hope for a miracle cure, hope for a release from pain, hope for the right doctor or healer, hope for spiritual enlightenment to transcend fear and suffering. Disguised as optimism, hope can sometimes be a form of denial. This is not to say that a cancer patient should surrender the commitment to healing, even in what may be the face of discouraging odds. Any adverse situation is more likely to be improved by a proactive, rather than a passive, stance. But the hope that leaves us waiting for some kind of redemption can be a drain on precious energies that could otherwise be used for coming to terms with our situation and exploring other possibilities for healing.

Linda and I were both so busy hoping for a cure for her metastatic cancer that we often neglected to focus on her healing. While these two words are often used interchangeably, they have very different meanings. A cure modifies aspects of the physical body to remove symptoms and suffering. The cure approach to illness and disease is the way of Western medicine. Healing—the root of the word means "whole"—is the process of restoring one's being to a state of wholeness, bringing peace to the soul. This is the intended outcome of most spiritual practice. In the beginning, Linda and I were focused on a cure. In terms of our relationship, the healing had already begun. It began the day the doctor gave us the news, the day I learned that we might not have much more time together.

I wanted Linda to go through as little discomfort as possible, and I wanted her body to be cured and to recover from cancer. But this desire was overshadowed by my longing to express my love to her by providing whatever care I could. I served Linda not just because I loved her, but because in doing so I felt at peace within myself. I did it because in doing so, there was no separation between the two of us, just the experience of connecting to each other, to ourselves, and to the truth of the present moment.

After the immediate effects of the second chemo cycle began to wear off, Linda's hair started falling out. At first we noticed some on the pillow and then gobs of it came out when she shampooed. Within days she had lost all her body hair in addition to her head hair. By conventional standards, Linda did look less attractive, even a bit strange. Yet despite her unique appearance, Linda looked beautiful to me, even more so than usual and I told her so. I also told her that I loved her more than ever, not because she needed my love but because it was true. Having been stripped of two of the things that Linda believed made her most attractive to me, an intact breast and a sexy full head of hair, she was now stripped naked and vulnerable in a way that I had never experienced her. Her vulnerable presence invoked from me a degree of compassion and love that I had previously felt toward her only in rare moments.

While the catalyst of Linda's crisis differed significantly from what I had endured in my depression, the underlying dynamics were identical. What was revealed to us both was the conditional and judgmental nature of our sense of self-worth. We had both associated deservedness of love and respect from people, including ourselves, with being successful in fulfilling certain requirements.

Although both Linda and I had trained in and practiced psychotherapy, the depth of these patterns was not illuminated until our bouts with depression and cancer. These experiences stripped us of the means on which we had become accustomed to relying to maintain our places in human society. With this disintegration of our social self, the fears lying beneath the surface of our awareness now rose our consciousness.

From my experience I knew the terror of being seen without the necessary props, of being at risk of the kind of rejection, humiliation, and forced isolation that I had spent much of my life trying to avert. Never in our lives had either Linda or I had the masks we hid behind ripped so totally from our faces. Only in direct confrontation with the deep feelings of unworthiness behind the mask could we find access to the healing that each of us craved.

While, for me, appreciating the gifts that Linda's health crisis contained was not too difficult, not surprisingly, it was harder for her to embrace this perspective. On an intellectual level, Linda could appreciate the lessons and opportunities contained in this crisis, but emotionally she hated it. She rebelled against the unfairness of her situation with unabashed outrage. Throughout the spring and into the summer, during the months of chemotherapy, we spent many nights lying awake, sometimes until dawn, while Linda raged and cried out her often-inconsolable feelings.

I came to understand and trust that Linda's cries were not expressions of denial or resistance that she needed to overcome and just accept the reality of the situation but, rather, were legitimate and honest expressions of her grief and pain. Although staying present in the full intensity of Linda's experience was not easy, I realized that her willingness to honor the kinds of feelings she had spent most of her life withholding or denying was an integral part of her healing process. It became clear to me that my job was not to remove her pain or quiet her mind, but to affirm the legitimacy of her feelings and her right to protest.

I didn't need to get Linda to express her feelings; they were speaking for themselves with or without my encouragement. She made it abundantly clear to me that she no longer was looking to me to make her life easier, safer, or more comfortable. It was just fine for me to resign from that job that we had both agreed years ago was mine. One of the many gifts that cancer had given her was the recognition of her right and responsibility to be true to herself and to honor all aspects of herself, even and particularly those that she had found unacceptable. Linda's healing into wholeness was no longer about being the person that she thought she needed to be to be acceptable to others but, rather, now was an unconditional acceptance of all aspects of herself. She didn't need my help to fulfill that mandate; she just needed me to get out of the way.

Providing this kind of support was something very new for me. I was accustomed to being a fixer, and for many years, Linda and I had colluded to make that my job, one with which I was not only familiar but also, as it turned out, very much attached to. "How do I 'do' *this* kind of support?" And since I had managed to get a fair amount of my self-esteem by being "useful" to Linda, I wondered where that would come from now.

It looked like there was going to be a learning curve for me as well as Linda. Fortunately, I would be given many opportunities to practice in the coming months and in the series of chemo sessions that followed, and the radiation treatments that followed that, and in supporting Linda in new ways as she more fully reentered the workplace with her newfound identity and her newly discovered commitment to living a life of unconditional authenticity.

Linda wasn't the only one who was liberated to honor her own truth at a much deeper level. I saw that we were both severely limited by our old programs. But being freed up for each of us to be ourselves was not without its own challenges and questions, one of which was, "What will be the glue that will bond us and keep us together now that the glue from our former system is gone?"

We soon found out that we had nothing to worry about.

Chapter 23

SACRED PARTNERSHIP

Linda

Today, I am committed to spending every day that Charlie and I are together being kind, caring, considerate and loving. There has been enough pain, fear, and suffering. I am determined to see how much beauty and love I can create. And every day, I say a prayer of gratitude for having my life, my health, a devoted husband, my children, grandchildren, friends, and work that I love.

I came to understand that some suffering in our relationship was preventable, and I became highly motivated to search out all those areas where I could make changes. There are still difficult topics that must be addressed, truths that must be spoken that are likely to cause discomfort, but the respect with which they are communicated allows them to be spoken without undue duress. We have co-created a relationship that is a holy sanctuary from the harshness that the larger world can often be.

The trust, cooperation, and closeness that we enjoy now results in bursts of creativity. One of these times, we escaped to Mendocino for a few days of vacation. It was hot as we climbed down the steep rock steps to the beach below, me in my skimpy bathing suit, barefoot, and carrying my heavy briefcase stuffed full of notes for brainstorming a relationships seminar. Settled on the sand, a gentle breeze blowing, we relaxed together and the course flowed out of our loving connection.

I was experiencing the zest, gusto, excitement, inter-connectedness, and a meeting of the hearts and minds that are characteristics of co-creativity. We were, as Ray Bradbury calls it, "tossing ideas like confetti." Basking in the deep delight of the joining of two visions and two voices, we were creating something new. In a matter of hours, we had the whole course designed.

For me, the co-creative process is a lot like lovemaking, starting with slow, gentle touches that became more passionate and heated as the ideas bounce back and forth, building on each other, holding a steady charge of excitement, and then culminating in a clear vision of what we want to create. Someone observing us would never suspect that not that long before our relationship had been in a state of siege, with hundreds of fights followed by protracted recoveries.

The state of trust and mutual respect was hard won, but we arrived in the magical zone where no distinction between work and play existed. It was a vacation day, and there was nothing in the world I'd rather be doing than creating a workshop with Charlie. With lots of laughter, pure enjoyment, and a deep mutual respect for the different contributions we each bring to the workshop's design, we forgot about time because we were so absorbed in the process. When we climbed back up the rock steps I was filled with a deep sense of satisfaction.

The image I hold of the intimacy stage of relationship is of Charlie and me standing across from each other, melting into each other's eyes. Laughing and crying for joy, we experience the bliss of connection. I am completely filled with love to overflowing and so turn to stand side by side, facing out into the world. In this turning to face the world, I made the transition from intimacy to the co-creative stage. At first the intensity of our energy had been contained inside our relationship. Now my understanding about love seeks a wider area of distribution. I feel compelled to take the understanding that we experience to move it out into the larger world, to touch others with the depth of our transformative love.

I lived to see the day when I receive all the love I desire; I'm stuffed to the gills. Participating in something transpersonal, larger than myself, gives me a sense of personal power, centeredness, connection, and understanding. The love I experience is so vast that the narrow channel must widen to allow that love to flow into the world.

I have come to understand that creativity is manifesting something that didn't exist before, and that co-creativity is joining with another to form something out of nothing. This process is a manifestation of the trust that continues to build between us. We could not go straight to the co-creative stage; we had to move through the earlier stages of our relationship first.

I experience co-creativity as a dynamic energy that motivates action and risk taking, as a connection to the deepest part of myself reaching out to connect to the deepest part of Charlie and others. The connection involves empathy and listening. I receive different levels of communication simul-taneously, a practical, logical understanding accompanied by intuitive knowing.

Co-creativity is fun. Enthusiasm prevails. It's stimulating, provocative, mind stretching, and absorbing, with the excite-ment of being on the edge of the precipice. This is a pleasurable, enlivening edge, anticipating continual surprise. It's here and now, in the moment, compelling me to pay attention. It's laughing, celebrating, and honoring what has been accomplished.

I'm not sure that I believe in the concept of marriages made in heaven. But when Charlie and I are in the magic, it's a tempting belief. From that vantage point, it's as though our souls were sent down to earth and guided to each other, as if guardian angels watched over us to make sure we didn't quit before we got the message of what we were supposed to be doing: to teach others how to heal and grow in their relationships. It is as though we were chosen as vehicles for the work.

Most of the time, I see us as ordinary people who slogged it out in the trenches like many others—no divine anything helping us, just dogged determination. Over the years, we kept doing our work as individuals and as a couple, until at a certain point we had finally done enough, and popped through to the co-creative stage. I hold a vision that if large numbers of people could reach the co-creative stage of relationship, we would live in a more peaceful world. In relationships characterized by this highest level of development, power is shared equally, and there is a consistent experience of living in love and joy.

Charlie and I have had transformative turning points in our lives in personal growth seminars. Charlie proposed marriage to me in a personal growth group, with a dozen members as witnesses. In another seminar, Charlie decided to change his career, which prompted our move to California. I began my journey as a group facilitator by facing my fear of public speaking the day I took the microphone to speak in front of two hundred people. Going to the couples' workshop in Oregon when we were on the verge of divorce was an epiphany for me, and I found the work I needed to do and the practices that helped save our marriage. And a seminar allowed Charlie, with the profound support of the entire group, to envision a fulfilling life outside the company and make up his mind to resign and come back to the family.

Knowing on a visceral level the transformative power of group dynamics, I dedicated my career to creating a context for others to dive deep inside themselves and experience the kind of breakthroughs I had. Offering seminars rooted in what Charlie and I had learned so far was the obvious next step.

After years of bumbling and stumbling, I was surprised to find myself in the role of the "ritual elder," guiding the process of transformation in others. Couples who are on the trans-formation path find their way to us, seeking the special knowl-edge we have acquired during our journey to wholeness.

If we want to achieve the highest level available in a relationship, challenges need to be endured and mastered. I shed the romantic notion that "if we love each other, the relationship will just flow." In our workshops, we attempt right away to break up any delusional thinking and romantic myths, letting participants know that having a great relationship is work—damn hard work at times. We say it often and in many ways.

Learning how to be present with these difficult emotions led me to a new depth of love. In the co-creative stage, I was able to comprehend the grand scheme of things. I discovered that all that I go through is an opportunity for my growth. It is a challenge to become stronger, wiser, more mature, and more loving.

By maintaining equanimity in the face of crisis, I am able to see with the broader vision. Having arrived at a place where I can stay open to what is, gives me a sense of great power. I feel courageous and capable, proud of being able to handle my life.

At times I experience great joy, wonder, and exhilaration in learning. Learning means accepting that sometimes I don't know. It means that sometimes, I have to be willing to be wrong about what I think is the way it is.

Every time I learn something my worldview and my perception shift in some way. I often thought that there was somebody out there with whom learning would be more comfortable. It took a while to let go of that fantasy and realize that it is not about finding the right person; it is about being the right person.

By becoming a dedicated student and a patient teacher, I am learning to ask the right questions. What are the qualities that originally drew me to my partner? Are they present now? What is the purpose of our relationship? How do we have a disagreement that neither of us loses? What is the most skillful way to handle my anger? What part of my own dark side have I not owned and am projecting onto my partner? What part of my golden side have I not owned and may be projecting onto my partner? How do we build trust back after it has fallen? What does it really mean to be responsible? What, for me, is compassionate self-care? If I were to lose my partner through divorce or death, what unfinished business would I have? What would be the areas of remorse and regret? How can I become a more loving person? My beloved, how may I best love you? What is my unique contribution to make in this world and in what way might my partner assist me in that process?

Living in questions like these allows me to be humble and bring an inquisitive mind to my relationship. Instead of being so full of righteous knowing, I am a good student of life, living in radical amazement, energized by the process of discovery. Wavy Gravy says, "Married life is a pit full of pitfalls, designed by some demonic deity for our conscious evolution." I do my work not only so that I can have more trust and better communication in my relationship and more enjoyment in the family. I also do the work to feel more whole.

In an old Sufi tale, a man named Nasrudin lived in the Middle East. He had the reputation of being a rascal, so at the border between the countries, the inspector had the guards search the saddlebags of Nasrudin's donkey caravan to see if he was smuggling gold or jewels. They found nothing.

Time passed, and Nasrudin came to the border with yet another donkey caravan. He was wearing a beautiful turban with a huge jewel and a robe of high-quality cloth. The inspector was more convinced than ever that Nasrudin was up to no good. He had the guards search everywhere, even inside the donkeys' mouths. Again, they found nothing. A year later, the inspector ran into Nasrudin in the bazaar. "Nasrudin, you rascal," he said. "Those times you crossed the border, I knew you were smuggling. I have no official capacity any longer. You can tell me what were you smuggling?" And Nasrudin answered, "Donkeys."

I love this story because it reminds me of the points in time that have such tremendous value and are so often overlooked. While we are searching for the jewels and gold, the peak experiences of our lives, the dramatic moments, we may overlook the mundane moments. Intimacy is often contained in ordinary gestures—a lingering gaze, a brief touch, a hug, and a gentle word of encouragement. It is all these donkey moments lined up that make for the riches.

In my life, I'm committed to having caravans of donkey moments each day: openhearted encounters with my beloved husband, with children, friends, clients, students, cats, plants in the garden, trees in my yard, and the sky. These moments make me feel wealthy.

I'm so glad I persevered. What I enjoy now is such a delight. I have more peace of mind than I have ever known. I feel a strong sense of trust in the relationship we have created and yet I do not take it for granted. Each one of the ordeals of my marriage made me stronger, first crushing me and then giving me new life. I learned so much about myself, about relationships, and about how the world works. The secret of life for me is about becoming a more loving person is clear. Also clear is that I had no way of doing that without developing my strength, courage, commitment, integrity, and personal power. It is through the ordeals of my life that I developed these qualities.

I'm especially glad to be giving my children and grand-children a model of a relationship that works, where there is a high level of respect, where power is shared, where there is strong trust, honesty, and vitality. They see love and devotion demonstrated daily. Our marriage not only gives them a secure environment for their own development but also an up-close prototype for their future sacred partnerships.

I know that when I am on my deathbed, the important question I will be asking myself is, "How well did I love?" I want to live my life now, every day, in such a way that I can answer, "I loved well; I loved fully; I loved many. I lived a life of devotion." I am making my little corner of the world a heaven on earth.

Chapter 24

WINDS OF GRACE

Grace: The state of being sanctified through freely bestowed divine love and protection.

Charlie

It's been said that whatever brings us to face the essential truth of our lives may be called "grace." Frequently, grace assumes a form that feels more like a curse than a blessing. It can be a life-threatening illness, the loss of a family member, being fired from a job, the kids leaving home (or coming back), divorce, a serious accident, or any number of possible crises that can be encountered in one's life.

It's often not until we go out of our mind with pain, terror, longing, rage, grief, confusion, or even joy, that experiencing the grace that liberates us from the tyranny of the fearful mind becomes possible. My year of depression and Linda's year of cancer treatment provided the grace that brought me to my knees. Although at the time I would have given anything to avoid these crises, I now see that the suffering I endured was a minuscule price to pay for benefits of the outcome. How can you quantify the value of freedom, inner peace, or the capacity to experience deep love? From my current perspective, I can't imagine any price that would be too high to pay for these gifts. Although at the time I would have given anything to avoid these ordeals, today I feel only gratitude.

These days gratitude permeates my feelings toward Linda. This feeling is very different from the guilt and dependence that I felt toward her while I was depressed. I have some sense now of how Linda suffered because of my unconsciousness and self-centeredness. I also have come to understand how my fear and unhealed wounds, rather than a basic flaw or deficiency within myself, drove my destructive actions. This recognition has helped me find forgiveness for myself and replace remorse and self-recrimination with acceptance and compassion, two qualities I can now more fully bring forth in my relationship with Linda and with others as well.

I am grateful to Linda for seeing in me that which I couldn't see in myself and for hanging in there even in the face of her own pain, despite well-intended advice from some of her friends to get out of the marriage. I am grateful for the vision that she held of a life very different from anything that we had known together, different even from anything that I imagined could be possible. Fortunately, Linda's vision was less limited than mine.

In the reality of the world that we share today, giving to Linda is giving to myself. The experience of sacrifice is one that is often present for me but not from a martyr's perspective. In the literal definition of the word, to sacrifice is to "make sacred." There is no feeling of loss on those occasions when I choose to forego my preferences in favor of Linda's, only a feeling of giving to myself by contributing to her happiness. I know and trust that she does the same for me. The days of keeping score as to whose turn it is to forego their preferences for the other are long gone.

Still we have times when our life together is something other than a blissful union. We continue to be very different people with different temperaments, dispositions, and points of view. Occasionally, differences arise that do not easily lend themselves to resolution, but I cannot remain angry for long, not because it is wrong but because I am no longer as able as I used to be to tolerate living with a closed heart. Differences rarely turn into conflicts anymore. Our commitment to working things out in a way that is both respectful and honest is an expression not of an obligation but, rather, of an understanding that to do otherwise causes harm to ourselves, as well as to each other. Although differences don't necessarily mean conflicts, they do have to be worked out. Sometimes this can be done simply by acknowledging their existence. We can agree to disagree, and quite often, we do.

This simple acknowledgment frequently represents the first step in a process leading to a deeper understanding. Being able to listen deeply and intently to each other has become more important to each of us than winning an argument or dominating the other. We are both becoming increasingly aware of the damage caused by relentless power struggles and the price that we each pay when we play to win rather than to understand.

What I consider to be one of the greatest feats that Linda and I have accomplished in our—now—forty-nine years together is not the resolution of our differences but the ability to live with those that seem irreconcilable. We've both discovered that even peace can have too high a price. Some things are worth fighting for, worth defending. If peace comes at the expense of one's dignity, self-respect, or integrity, it is no peace at all, merely an uneasy truce that at some point will inevitably break down. Knowing how to relate skillfully and respectfully, even amid heated emotions, and when to let go is an essential skill for any meaningful relationship. We've both learned a lot about this distinction over the years.

From time to time, participants in our workshops have expressed concern that without the struggle for dominance that characterizes most marriages, things might get boring. I tell them that our relationship is anything but boring. Linda and I are continually confronting the question, "How can we make this work even better for both of us?" And neither of us is willing to settle for anything less. Rather than relating to each other as adversaries vying for scarce resources, something we did for many years, we each value the other's happiness as much as our own. If anything is boring and unexciting, it is being stuck in the repetitive, defensive postures that lead to replaying predictable and frustrating scenarios.

The connection that Linda and I now share is so close that we can sometimes read each other's minds and know each other's feelings without a word being spoken. The irony is that through this remarkably intimate connection, I experience a degree of personal freedom that is unprecedented in my life. The trust that Linda and I now share has enabled each of us to release the many forms of control we exercised over each other in the past. In the absence of the manipulative strategies bred of our own insecurity, a place of enormous spaciousness has opened within each of us and between us. This opening is the place where freedom and commitment meet.

In the past, my love for Linda had been tainted and diminished by the guilt and resentment that are the by-products of codependent relationships. Out of the private and shared hells that we experienced, both Linda and I found parts of ourselves that we had previously disowned or were unaware of. As I came to terms with these hidden aspects of myself, Linda and I became less polarized in our needs for connection and separateness. As I acknowledged my need for closeness and found the courage to risk being emotionally vulnerable with Linda, she became more accepting of her own shadow side, including the parts of her that valued privacy, separateness, and solitude. As we each became more whole, our dependence on each other to bring each of us into balance diminished, as did the resentment and fear that accompanies any relationship in which each person holds the power for the other's sense of well-being.

It wasn't until both Linda and I found ourselves through the lessons of our ordeals that our marriage became truly loving. As we each have healed into our wholeness, our capacity for love has grown. I am now not only more able to give more selflessly to Linda, but I am also able to receive the gifts she bestows on me more graciously. I feel worthy of accepting her offerings in the many forms in which they come: a special gift when there's no occasion or "reason" for it, a favorite dish lovingly prepared, an unsolicited "I love you," an unexpected backrub, a compliment, encouragement to take time for myself, and hundreds of other presents that seem to be constantly coming my way.

I also feel worthy of giving to Linda, and I take pleasure in coming up with new and creative ways of surprising her with unexpected delights. I no longer give to her out of a sense of duty, guilt, or obligation. I give out of a deep desire to express my love. I give because I am no longer consumed by buried resentment and unmet expectations. I give out of the joy that I experience in Linda's happiness. I give because I am enlarged, not diminished, in this process, and my gifts to her are gifts to myself.

Taking delight in the process of giving has strengthened my capacity for generosity in general. In becoming more generous I have found my level of trust in myself, as well as in the world, has grown and deepened. I find myself less concerned with getting and more confident that my needs will all be met, although not necessarily without effort on my part, and not always on my terms.

I have discovered a strange paradox in the process of learning about the power of generosity. As I learned to put aside self-interest to more deeply attune to Linda's reality, I have experienced a more satisfying kind of well-being than that which comes from the fulfillment of egoistic desires. Until I was thrust out of my self-centered cocoon, I wasn't able to experience the fulfillment of my deeper longings. Then I was addicted to the need to seek gratification of the superficial wants that kept me empty because my heart was mostly closed.

It's been humbling and at times embarrassing to recognize the degree to which I have compulsively sought the pleasures of the senses and the ego. Looking good, feeling good, and being right were for most of my life my priorities, even—perhaps particularly—when I was pontificating from the front of the room about selfless service. These pleasures pale in comparison to the experience of authentic openheartedness. Even during those times when there is pain, there is a kind of richness in opening oneself to the truth of the moment, whatever it is.

Although at times I had tasted joy of this kind, it took a crisis to show me that the experience was available to me every time I subordinated my personal preferences to a purpose greater than myself. During Linda's healing, I had many opportunities to practice this kind of giving. In the process of attuning myself more attentively to Linda, I have become less concerned with fulfilling my own desires, while paradoxically feeling more fulfilled. I haven't lost my interest in doing the things that had previously brought me pleasure; I simply lost my compulsivity and control around these activities and desires.

Being with Linda has become one of the things that I want to do. It seems she has changed and become less demanding, less needy, less insecure than she was, and I feel more drawn to her than I have since the early days of our relationship. Shaken out of her own life-numbing patterns by all our ordeals, Linda has become a different person, one who knows that life is too short to waste time indulging in self-pity, smoldering resentment, and passivity. The fire that cancer lit beneath her seems to be growing hotter all the time, burning away the remaining vestiges of her resistance to life.

Linda wears her power with grace and authority and no longer seems to feel threatened by the power of others. I find myself feeling drawn to the vitality she exudes, and I find her passion for life alluring and engaging. Although her body lacks some of the physical tone that it used to have, as far as I'm concerned, she's never been sexier. It is the fullness of her overall being and how present she can now be, unencumbered by the worries and anxieties that used to plague her. She is much less dependent on me, yet she is not fully self-contained.

At the same time, she is deeply connected to her own life and to all life around her. Our relationship has become one place in the larger continuum of life on which Linda's need for intimacy is fulfilled rather than the one and only source of that experience.

Friendships have become more important as Linda and I have each grown less dependent on each other. Paradoxically, as we have each strengthened our connections with others, our relationship has become more fulfilling. I used to enjoy an aspect of being needed by Linda. Her dependence on me made me feel special and secure. I knew that she wasn't likely to go anywhere if I was the one with the power to make her happy. Over time, however, what had felt reassuring began to feel suffocating. In part, my need to escape the oppressiveness of a constricted marriage led me to a job that took me away from home as many as three weeks a month for more than five years.

I currently have several good friends with whom I spend time regularly. Because of my work with men, I've discovered the value of real male friendship and learned something about creating the kinds of relationships with men in which genuine intimacy and radical honesty are both possible. Another part of me is expressed and nurtured in the presence of these men than when I am with Linda or in the company of women. We each need input from both men and women to support and keep in balance our masculine and feminine aspects. My men's group has been a great source of enormous support and inspiration to me for many years.

My marriage has become a sacred partnership in which our shared purpose is no longer primarily the seeking of emotional or sexual gratification. Rather, it is an arena in which we can extend the love that is generated between us to include others as well. Our children and grandchildren have been the most immediate benefactors and contributors to this process. Witnessing the metamorphosis of our home from a place of heartache and suffering into a loving sanctuary has been for me the most miraculous part of this transformation. The emotional climate of our home is currently characterized by laughter, respect, and warmth.

We have a significantly lowered threshold for the discord and conflict that we used to see as "normal" for a family. What were previously rationalized as legitimate forms of self-expression were actually cries of pain from unresolved discord and unmet needs. What I had justified as vitality and passion had more to do with the drama and intensity that arise from a state of prolonged unhappiness and resignation. The distress that had been the norm in the family is now the exception, and our intolerance for avoidable distress has become a powerful motivator for the resolution of our differences. We have all, to a large degree, recovered from the desensitization that came from living in an emotionally volatile or unstable environment.

The effects of the foundation of stability that Linda and I have built have spilled over to other systems of our lives: family, extended family, work, and community. I no longer focus on the "deficiencies" and "shortcomings" of others and focus, instead, on doing my own work. In diverting my attention from my judgment of other people, the problematic aspects of their personalities seem to disappear. It isn't that everyone else is changing but that I am no longer viewing others from the vantage point of what's wrong with them. Underestimating the power of this shift toward self-responsibility rather than trying to correct others is impossible.

As I have become less inclined to be critical or controlling in my relationships, others are more open and expressive of their feelings with me. Jesse told me a few years ago, when I was receptive enough to finally hear what he had to say, that what I had intended to be helpful and supportive advice felt to him like harsh criticism and a mistrust of his intelligence and abilities. When I told him that I didn't feel that way and asked him why he never told me that before, he said, "Why would I? You wouldn't have listened." He was right.

The great Indian saint Sri Ramakrishna reminds us that "the winds of Grace are always blowing, we need only raise our sails." Grace is that which provides me access to my own true nature. Sometimes that includes the recognition of painful or difficult truths. In opening myself to receive the full intensity of the feelings that emerged with the crises of my depression, I found myself feeling more fully alive than I'd been before, not just because I wanted to be but because experiencing anything other than that was impossible for me. Life crises can cut like a knife through layers of defensiveness and conditioned resistance to life itself, dissolving the patterns that insulate us from being overwhelmed by unmanageable conditions and feelings. My real challenge has not been to become more adept at limiting the intensity of my feeling but to keep the sails open, even when the velocity of the wind increases. In learning to do this, I am becoming more able to develop the strength that is necessary to stand in the presence of the truth of each unfolding moment, regardless of what that may be.

The truth of the moment before me right now is that I don't know. I've learned so much over the course of the sweet and tumultuous times of our marriage, yet the lesson that stands out for me is that I just don't know. I don't know how much more time Linda and I have left to spend together. I don't know how we made it through hell. I don't know what other challenges await me and who I will become in the process of meeting them. I don't know why I'm so lucky and what I've done to deserve it.

One of the very few things that I do know is that there are some things that are more important than knowing, and this is what Linda has taught me: that matters of the heart are no less important than matters of the mind. She's known this her whole life. I used to know it, forgot it, and then remembered again. Who knows? I may forget again. If I do, I've at least had this time, this sweet precious time, brief though it may be, in which I was sailing a ship called *Grace,* and the winds were filling the billowing sail.

Acknowledgments

To Wendy Jo Dymond and Stephanie Marohn, whose editing skills enhanced the quality of our manuscript immeasurably. A thousand thank-yous!

And to our readers and colleagues, Marcia Naomi Berger, Leisa Creo, Mary Amrita Arden, Alanna Brogan, David Kerns, Susan Campbell, Gary Fagin, Gregg Levoy, Renee Trudeau, David Lustig, Daphne Rose Kingma, Maya Spector, Barry and Joyce Vissell, Roberta Valdez, Lynn Gallo, Carolyn Levering, and John and Deo Robbins, who gave so much of yourselves through your time, thoughtfulness and penetrating, respectful feedback. Your input has been invaluable to us.

And to our office manager and right-hand woman Tiffanie Luna, for believing in us and in our work and whose support, steadiness, and technical expertise, provided us with the support that we needed even when we didn't know that we needed it.

To our publisher, Sharon Lund at Sacred Life Publishers, who had faith in us and in our project and provided great support along the way.

And to Ondrea Levine, who connected us with Sharon Lund and for the source of inspiration that she's been to us since our first meeting in 1984.

To our dear friend and trickster-in-chief Doug Von Koss, who we have always been able to count on to keep us from taking things too seriously.

We also want to acknowledge some of our most influential teachers who offered us great wisdom and profound teachings through their writings, their teachings, and by being a living embodiment of their principles: Seymour and Sylvia Boorstein, John and Julie Gottman, Ram Dass, Thich Nhat Hanh, Gary Chapman, Gay and Kathlyn Hendricks, Jack Kornfield, Jiddu Krishnamurti, Harville Hendrix, Robert Bly, and Marion Woodman.

And to the many learning centers throughout the country that have sponsored our seminars and workshops, particularly the Esalen Institute in Big Sur California where we have been facilitating seminars since 1995, and the Kripalu Center for Yoga and Health in Lenox, Massachusetts, where we have taught for over ten years. Thank you for believing in our work!

And to our children, who have brought so much joy and so many "growth opportunities" into our lives, we are deeply grateful. And indescribable gratitude for the brilliant light that your children, Devin, Ashton, and Seth bring to us. It's through them that we are inspired to work to fulfill our vision of a world in which peace, love, truthfulness, and integrity are the values that prevail and inform the lives of all people.

And to the students and clients who have inspired us with your courage, commitment, and vulnerability. Thank you for your willingness to dare to free yourselves from the security of your defensiveness in your quest to live a more wholehearted life.

And last, we dedicate this book to Stephen Levine, our friend and mentor (although he may not have known it) who passed away as the final draft of this book was being completed and who gently coaxed us both into minding our own business and doing our own work, even when it was so obvious what the other needed to do. Thank you for your patience, your sense of humor, your beautiful smile, and your unrelenting faith in us and in all human beings, to be able to keep our hearts open, even in hell. Without that, this book could never have been written.

About the Authors

Linda Bloom, LCSW, and Charlie Bloom, MSW, have been assisting individuals, couples, and organizations in the process of enhancing the quality of their relationships since 1975. The founders and co-directors of *Bloomwork*, they have lectured and taught seminars on relationships since 1986 to thousands of people throughout the United States and in many other countries.

The Blooms are regular presenters at the Esalen Institute, the Kripalu Center for Yoga & Health, 1440 Multiversity, and Rancho La Puerta. They have also served as adjunct faculty members and lecturers at the California Institute of Integral Studies, the Institute of Imaginal Studies, the California School of Professional Psychology, the University of California Berkeley Extension Program, Antioch University, the Omega Institute, John F. Kennedy University, and many other institutions of higher learning. They are bloggers for several online journals, including the *Huffington Post, Psychology Today, Psych Central, Blogger.com, Tumblr, GuideDoc, and OMTimes.*

Charlie and Linda have been married since 1972. They live in Northern California. They are the parents of two grown children, Jesse and Sarah, and grandparents of Devin, Ashton, and Seth.

Contact information and much more about Charlie and Linda and their work is available on their website, *www.bloomwork.com.*

OTHER BOOKS BY

CHARLIE AND LINDA BLOOM

101 Things I Wish I Knew When I Got Married: Simple Lessons to Make Love Last

Secrets of Great Marriages: Real Truth from Real Couples about Lasting Love

Happily Ever After. . . and 39 Other Myths about Love